Victory in the Opening

by IM Gary Lane

B.T.Batsford Ltd, *London*

First published in 1999
© Gary Lane 1999

ISBN 0 7134 8546 9

British Library Cataloguing-in-Publication Data.
A catalogue record for this book is
available from the British Library.

Printed in Great Britain by
Creative Print & Design (Wales), Ebbw Vale
for the publishers,
B.T.Batsford Ltd,
583 Fulham Road,
London SW6 5BY

A BATSFORD CHESS BOOK
General Manager: Nigel Davies
Advisors: Mark Dvoretsky, Raymond Keene OBE,
Daniel King, Jon Speelman, Chris Ward

Contents

Dedicated to Nancy Jones

I would like to thank François Mertens for his help in producing this book.

Symbols used

+	check
+-	winning advantage for White
±	large advantage for White
+=	slight advantage for White
-+	winning advantage for Black
∓	large advantage for Black
=+	slight advantage for Black
=	level position
!	good move
!!	outstanding move
!?	interesting move
?!	dubious move
?	bad move
??	blunder
1-0	the game ends in a win for White
0-1	the game ends in a win for Black
½-½	the game ends in a draw

Introduction

The main aim of this book is to show how to punish unusual, indifferent or mistaken moves in the opening by taking swift and appropriate action. So often, when faced with a bad move, players will just carry on blindly with their normal plan and thereby miss out on a decisive winning chance.

The opening tussles presented here are all decided within 25 moves and provide a wide range of tactical ideas designed to create maximum difficulties for your opponent at a very early stage of the game. You will have to look elsewhere for deep theoretical innovations on move twenty or so—the examples here, all taken from practical play, are effectively decided well before then! Indeed, by familiarising yourself with some of the many tricks and traps contained in the openings it should be possible for you to win many more games quickly and incisively. Moreover, with three diagrams on each page, you can even follow the games from beginning to end without the need of a chess set, thus making it an ideal travelling companion.

Chapter One deals with 'Greedy Openings', which highlights the necessity of knowing where to sacrifice material and, equally importantly, when to accept it. It can be a difficult learning curve, especially when your opponent's queen is busy snatching your pawns and all you can remember is that the book said you had compensation—but did not tell you why! Here the illustrative games are very valuable because they tell the full story of how a sustained initiative generated by rapid piece development can lead to a quick victory.

If you cherish hopes of winning a fantastic game in dramatic fashion then the chapter 'Chasing the King' is for you. All the conditions necessary for launching a successful king-hunt are laid down, together with brilliant practical examples of how to conduct the attack. Identification of recurring patterns, such as critical weaknesses in the opponent's defensive pawn shield, will alert the experienced chess tournament campaigner to possibilities of ambushing the enemy king.

'Keeping all options open' is the slogan of those players brave enough to defer castling. Though leaving the king in the centre until the middlegame might enable a player to castle on the opposite wing to where an opponent shows aggressive intentions, there is the drawback that such an uncastled king interferes with the coordination of the rooks, thus resulting in an overall lack of harmony of one's forces.

'Attacking the King in the Centre' looks at the consequences of not being able to castle. Typical examples show powerful methods of exploitation and execution on the board.

'Attacking the Castled King' offers various techniques which more often than not result in the destruction of the enemy pawn cover. Our illustrative games feature popular methods of attack such as opening lines and diagonals, the pawn storm, manoeuvring and probing for weaknesses. How to handle opposite-side castling is also explained with a particular emphasis on timing—a crucial factor in determining which attack arrives first.

'Checkmate in the Opening' presents a feast of games with a strong tactical slant. The king is hounded at every opportunity and a number of typical mates are demonstrated.

'Winning Moves' sounds like the answer to all our problems. Surprisingly, the fact that the games tend to be spectacular is more the result of a well thought out plan rather than spontaneous inspiration. So here you have the opportunity to sharpen up your tactical awareness as well as to implement familiar attacking themes.

There will be times when you will be obliged to transpose into an endgame with many hours of tedious manoeuvring in prospect. But not always! The chapter 'Opening to the Ending' shows that this final phase of the game may *not* be slow and strategic in nature, but tactical. In such cases it may be a positive advantage to head straight for the ending.

'Opening Surprises' looks at unusual continuations designed to confuse and upset your opponent. Here you are handed an arsenal of opening tricks, backed up by logical analysis, to help you score an early victory.

The serious consequences of not activating one's pieces is a theme which we have seen again and again. However, our final chapter, 'Lack of Development' is dedicated solely to this topic. It is clear, after looking at a few games illustrating the attacking possibilities, that the task of organising a defence with half of one's pieces still on their original squares is a recipe for disaster.

Throughout the book, the selection of openings and games has been governed by their likelihood of appearing in practical play—and with an emphasis on decisive action taking place within only ten moves.

1 Greedy Openings

'I can resist anything but temptation' is the quote which comes to mind in Greedy Openings. The bait of a pawn or a piece is often enough for players to lose their senses and forget about basic principles. Games where a big advantage in development is gained as a result of an opponent grabbing material in the opening continue to be seen time and again.

A significant advantage in development can be a deadly force. Even grandmasters are not immune to this danger. In Browne-Quinteros, Black goes pawn hunting in the opening and after twelve moves has only his queen in play while White has mobilised virtually his entire army. The end comes swiftly with White ripping open the centre to get at Black's uncastled king.

In the game Onischuk-Hertneck, Black tries his luck with an obscure line of the French. Once again the queen goes on walkabout in pursuit of material gain but this leaves his queenside undeveloped and unable to form a reasonable defence. Inevitably, Black pays a heavy price for his indulgence.

Keres-Spassky provides an example of calculated risk from top class chess. Keres offers material, not for any immediate return but for lasting pressure. This kind of material investment requires fine judgement and is probably the most difficult to apply in practical play. Keres's conduct of the game is most instructive.

Then again, it can happen that a player will grab a pawn or piece and simply hang on to it and win! The game Dougherty-Hergott will make you think twice before employing an opening which sacrifices a pawn after a mere two moves. Also the idea of throwing all your pieces into one massive attack sounds great but the game Illescas-Anand issues a cautionary warning that such an attack doesn't always come off. Black jumps at the chance to snatch material and lives to tell the tale.

French: 3 ... ♘e4
Onischuk-Hertneck
Biel 1997

1 e4 e6 2 d4 d5 3 ♘d2 ♘f6 4 e5 ♘e4

A popular way to avoid main line theory. The position can also arise after 3 ♘c3 ♘f6 4 e5 ♘e4.

5 ♘xe4

Onischuk rightly wants to give Black a weak pawn on e4. Instead Agnos-Rice, Port Erin 1997, continued 5 ♗d3 ♘xd2 6 ♗xd2 c5 7 c3 ♕b6 8 ♘f3 ♘c6=.

5 ... dxe4 6 ♗c4 c5 7 d5

An aggressive continuation which directly challenges the soundness of Black's opening choice.

7 ... ♕b6?!

The one-move threat of 8 ... ♕b4+ allows Black to adopt an unusual set-up. Also:

a) 7 ... ♘d7 8 dxe6 fxe6 9 ♘h3! ♘xe5 10 ♕h5+ ♘f7 11 ♘g5 g6 12 ♕g4 h5 13 ♗b5+ ♚e7 14 ♕f4 ♘d6 15 ♕e5 ♗h6 16 ♘xe4 ♘xe4 17 ♗xh6 1-0 Dvoirys-Florath, Berlin 1996.

b) 7 ... exd5 8 ♕xd5 ♕xd5 9 ♗xd5 ♘d7 10 ♗f4 f5 11 exf6 ♘xf6 12 0-0-0+=.

8 c3 ♘d7 9 f4! exd5

9 ... exf3!? helps White to develop with 10 ♘xf3.

10 ♕xd5 ♕g6 11 ♘e2 ♗e7

Or 11 ... ♕xg2? 12 ♕xf7+ ♚d8 13 ♖g1 ♕xh2 14 ♗e3 ♗e7 15 0-0-0+-.

12 ♘g3 ♗h4 13 0-0 ♗xg3 14 hxg3 0-0 15 f5 ♕xg3 16 ♗f4 ♕g4 17 e6!

White triumphs with panache.

17 ... fxe6 18 fxe6 ♘b6 19 e7+!! ♘xd5 20 exf8=♕+ ♚xf8 21 ♗d6+ ♚e8 22 ♗b5+ ♗d7 23 ♖f8 mate.

after 4 ... ♘e4

after 7 d5

after 17 e6

Sicilian: 3 ♗b5+
Browne-Quinteros
Wijk aan Zee 1974

1 e4 c5 2 ♘f3 d6 3 ♗b5+ ♗d7 4 ♗xd7+ ♕xd7 5 c4 ♕g4?!

5 0-0 is considered the main line. Now Black tries to take advantage of White's 5th by grabbing a pawn.

6 0-0 ♕xe4 7 d4 cxd4 8 ♖e1

Logically gaining time with an attack on the queen. In Bates-Williams, Witley 1998, White took the pawn immediately with 8 ♘xd4 There followed 8 ... ♘f6 9 ♘c3 ♕g4 10 ♕a4+ ♕d7 11 ♘db5 ♘c6 12 ♖e1 e5 which led to a draw after 21 moves.

8 ... ♕c6

In Bologan-Paranichev, USSR Team Championship 1988, Black experimented with 8 ... ♕g4 and came under enduring pressure. The game continued 9 h3 ♕d7 10 ♘xd4 ♘c6 11 ♘c3 e6 12 ♗f4 ♖d8 13 ♕d3 ♗e7 14 ♖ad1 ♘f6 15 ♘db5 0-0 16 ♕f3 ♘e8 17 ♗xd6! ♗xd6 18 c5 ♕e7 19 cxd6 ♘xd6 20 ♘d5 ♕d7 21 ♘xd6 exd5 22 ♖xd5+=.

9 ♘xd4 ♕xc4

9 ... ♕d7 is a more practical choice but White has plenty of play after 10 ♘b5.

10 ♘a3 ♕c8 11 ♗f4 ♕d7 12 ♘ab5 e5

Quinteros's backward development encourages White to rip open the centre.

13 ♗xe5 dxe5 14 ♖xe5+ ♗e7

14 ... ♘e7 15 ♘f5 f6 16 ♘fd6+ ♔d8 17 ♘xb7+ wins or 14 ... ♔d8 15 ♕f3 ♘f6 16 ♖d1 ♔c8 17 ♘b3+-.

15 ♖d5 ♕c8 16 ♘f5 ♔f8 17 ♘xe7 ♔xe7 18 ♖e5+ 1-0

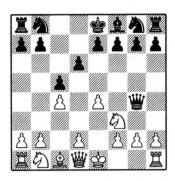

after 5 ... ♕g4

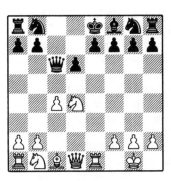

after 9 ♘d4

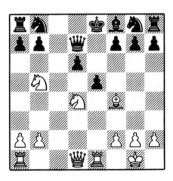

after 12 ... e5

Nimzo-Indian: 4 e3 ♘e4
Aleksandrov-Sulskis
New York 1998

1 d4 ♘f6 2 c4 e6 3 ♘c3 ♗b4 4 e3 ♘e4!?

This direct approach has been ignored for years in favour of more flexible options such as 4 ... b6, 4 ... c5 and 4 ... 0-0.

5 ♕c2

Other possibilities are:

a) 5 ♕g4 ♘xc3 6 a3 ♗e7 7 bxc3 0-0 with equal chances.

b) 5 ♘ge2 ♕f6 6 f3 ♘xc3 7 ♘xc3 c5 8 d5 ♗xc3+ 9 bxc3 ♕xc3+?! 10 ♗d2 ♕f6 11 ♗d3 exd5 12 cxd5 ♕g5 13 0-0 ♕xd5 14 ♗c3 c4 15 ♗e2 ♕xd1 16 ♖fxd1 0-0 17 ♗xc4 gave White a stranglehold on the position in Komjenovic-Meana Fernandez, Dos Hermanas 1998.

5 ... f5 6 ♗d3 0-0 7 ♘ge2 b6

A distinct improvement on 7 ... d5 which was played in Reshevsky-Kramer, USA Ch 1957, which continued: 7 ... d5 8 a3 ♗xc3+ 9 bxc3 b6 10 cxd5 exd5 11 c4 dxc4 12 ♗xc4+ ♔h8 13 ♘f4 c6 14 a4 ♘d6 15 ♗b3 a5 16 h4 ♖e8 17 ♗b2 b5 18 d5 ♘c4 19 ♗xc4±.

8 0-0 ♗xc3 9 ♗xe4 fxe4 10 ♘xc3 d5 11 b4 ♘c6 12 ♕b3 ♗a6 13 ♕a4

Aleksandrov is hoping for the passive 13 ... ♗b7.

13 ... ♗xc4!

Black abandons material in search of a lightning attack.

14 ♕xc6 ♗xf1 15 ♕xe6+ ♔h8 16 ♔xf1 ♕h4 17 ♘d1 ♖xf2+! 0-1

Checkmate will quickly follow: 18 ♘xf2 ♖f8 19 ♔e1 ♕xf2+ 20 ♔d1 ♕f1+ 21 ♔c2 ♕d3+ 22 ♔b2 ♖f2+.

after 4 ... ♘e4

after 13 ♕a4

after 17 ♘d1

Latvian Gambit: 4 ... ♛g5
Repp-Paschitta
Correspondence game 1991

1 e4 e5 2 ♘f3 f5 3 ♗c4 fxe4 4 ♘xe5 ♛g5

An outrageous attempt by Black to capture as much material as possible and then try to survive the resulting onslaught.

5 d4 ♛xg2 6 ♛h5+ g6 7 ♗f7+ ♚d8

In Kozlov-Svendsen, Correspondence 1991, Black tried another square for his king with 7 ... ♚e7. That game went 8 ♗g5+! ♘f6 9 ♛h4 ♛xh1+ 10 ♚d2 e3+ 11 ♚e2 ♗g7 12 ♘c3 ♛g2 13 ♘e4! ♚f8 14 ♗xf6 g5 15 ♛h5 ♛xe4 16 ♗xg7+ ♚xg7 17 ♛xg5+ and the reward for Black's inventive play was a lost position.

8 ♗xg6 ♛xh1+ 9 ♚e2 c6 10 ♘c3 e3

Eager to win more material. Or:

a) 10 ... ♛g2 11 ♘f7+ ♚c7 12 ♗xe4 ♛g7 13 ♘xh8 ♘f6 14 ♛f7± Pavlanin-Sladek, Czech Team Championship 1995.

b) 10 ... ♘f6 11 ♛g5 ♖g8 12 ♛xf6+ ♗e7 13 ♛f7 ♖f8 14 ♛xf8 ♗xf8 15 ♗g5+ ♚c7 16 ♖xh1 hxg6 17 ♘xg6 gave White a winning ending in Grava-Budovskis, Correspondence 1970.

11 ♘f7+ ♚c7 12 ♗xe3 ♛xa1 13 ♛g5 ♗e7 14 ♗f4+ ♚b6

Or 14 ... d6 15 ♗d6+ ♚d7 16 ♛f5+ mating.

15 ♘a4+ ♚a6 16 ♗d3+ b5 17 ♘c5+ ♚b6 18 ♘d6 ♘a6 19 ♘c4+!

The harmonious positions of White's forces encourage a glorious finish.

19 ... bxc4 20 ♘a4+ ♚b7 21 ♛b5+! cxb5 22 ♗e4+ 1-0

after 4 ... ♛g5

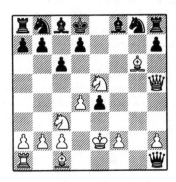

after 10 ♘c3

after 18 ... ♘a6

Queen's Indial: 4 ... ♗a6 5 ♘bd2
Adorjan-Kudrin
New York 1987

**1 d4 ♘f6 2 ♘f3 e6 3 c4 b6 4 g3
♗a6 5 ♘bd2**

5 b3 is more natural but the text contains a certain amount of venom. 5 ♕b3 is considered in the illustrative game Epishin-Komarov in the chapter 'Opening to the Ending'.

5 ... ♗b7 6 ♗g2 c5 7 e4 cxd4

7 ... ♘xe4? leads to calamity. For instance: 8 ♘e5 d5 (8 ... ♘c3 9 ♕h5! g6 10 ♕h3+-) 9 cxd5 exd5 10 ♕a4+! ♘d7 11 ♘xe4 dxe4 12 ♗h3 ♗c8 13 ♕c6 ♖b8 14 ♘xf7+-.

8 e5 ♘g4

Kudrin seeks to undermine the e5 pawn. Other replies are:

a) 8 ... ♘g8 9 0-0 ♕c7 10 ♘xd4 ♗xg2 11 ♔xg2 a6 12 ♕f3 ♘c6 13 ♘xc6 dxc6 14 ♘e4 ♖c8 15 ♗f4 ♗e7 16 ♖ad1+= Bellon Lopez-Gamarra Caceres, Lucerne Olympiad 1982.

b) 8 ... ♘e4 9 ♘xe4 (9 0-0!?) 9 ... ♗xe4 10 ♕xd4 ♗b4+ 11 ♗d2 ♗xf3 12 ♗xf3 ♘c6 13 ♗xc6 ♗xd2+ 14 ♕xd2 dxc6 15 ♖d1 ♕xd2+ 16 ♖xd2 ½-½ J.Bellin-Copeland, British League 1998.

9 0-0 ♕c7 10 ♖e1 ♗c5?! 11 ♘e4! d3 12 ♘fg5! ♘xe5 13 ♗f4

This irritating pin is the price Black must pay for taking the two pawns.

13 ... d6 14 ♕h5 ♔f8 15 ♘xc5 bxc5 16 ♖xe5 dxe5 17 ♗xe5 ♕d7 18 ♗xb7 ♕xb7 19 ♘xe6+! ♔g8

If 19 ... fxe6 then 20 ♗d6+ ♔g8 21 ♕e8 mate.

20 ♘xg7 ♘c6 21 ♘f5! ♘xe5 22 ♕g5+ ♘g6 23 ♕f6 1-0

after 5 ♘bd2

after 8 e5

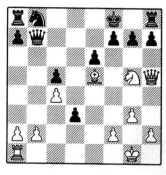

after 18 ... ♕xb7

Sicilian: Wing Gambit
Dougherty-Hergott
Toronto 1998

1 e4 c5 2 b4

The Wing Gambit has a good pedigree having been adopted in the 1920s by Marshall and Spielmann.

2 ... cxb4 3 a3 d5

This counterattacking move deprives White of much of his fun. Having accepted the offer of a pawn, Black does not greedily capture another but proceeds to stake a claim in the centre. In Fantini-Baccarin Viaro, Pan-American Championship 1996, Black took the pawn with 3 ... bxa3 which enabled White's pawns to dominate the centre. The game continued: 4 ♘xa3 d6 5 d4 ♘d7 6 ♘f3 e6 7 ♗d3 ♘gf6 8 0-0 ♗e7 9 ♕e2 0-0 10 ♗b2 a6 11 c4 b6 12 e5 dxe5 13 dxe5 ♘e8 14 ♕e4+-.

4 exd5 ♕xd5 5 ♗b2

Also possible:

a) 5 axb4?? ♕e5+ 0-1 Shirazi-Peters, USA Ch 1984.

b) 5 ♘f3 e5 6 axb4 ♗xb4 7 c3 ♗e7 8 ♘a3 ♘f6 9 ♘b5 ♕d8 10 ♘xe5 ♘c6= Lutz-De Firmian, Biel 1993.

5 ... e5 6 axb4 ♗xb4 7 ♘a3 ♘f6 8 ♘f3 0-0 9 ♗e2 ♘c6 10 ♘c4 e4

Hergott is clearly on top. White is running out of decent squares for his pieces and the king remains stuck in the centre.

11 ♘fe5 ♘xe5 12 ♘xe5 ♖d8 13 ♘c4 ♕g5 14 ♔f1

If 14 0-0 then 14 ... ♗h3 15 ♘e3 ♗xd2 wins.

14 ... ♗e6 15 c3 ♗xc4 0-1

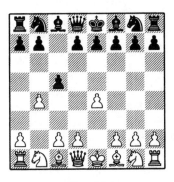

after 2 b4

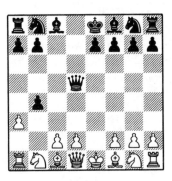

after 4 ... ♕xd5

after 10 ... e4

Nimzo-Indian: 4 e3, 6 ... ♘e4
Keres-Spassky
*Game Eight, Candidates Match,
Riga 1965*

**1 d4 ♘f6 2 c4 e6 3 ♘c3 ♗b4 4
e3 b6 5 ♗d3 ♗b7 6 ♘f3 ♘e4 7 0-0**
Keres offers a pawn in return for
attacking opportunities.

7 ... ♗xc3
The challenge is accepted. Other
replies:

a) 7 ... f5 8 d5 ♗xc3 9 bxc3 ♘c5
10 ♗a3 ♘ba6 11 ♗c2 (11 ♖e1 ♕f6
12 ♕c2 g6 13 e4 fxe4 14 ♗xe4
0-0-0 15 ♘d2+= Sadler-Ward,
Hastings 1997) 11 ... ♕f6 12 ♘d4
0-0 13 f3 g6 14 ♕d2 e5 15 ♖f2 d6
16 ♘e2 ♘d7 17 ♔h1 ♘ac5 18 ♖g1
♗a6=+ Buckley-Ward, British
Championship 1998.

b) 7 ... ♘xc3 8 bxc3 ♗xc3 9 ♖b1
♘c6 10 ♖b3 ♗a5 11 e4! h6 12 ♗b2
♘b4 13 ♗b1 ♗a6 14 a3 ♘c6 15
♕c2 ♘e7 16 d5 ♖g8 17 ♖d1 c5 18
dxe6 fxe6 19 ♘e5 d6 20 ♖f3 ♕c7
21 ♕a4+ b5 22 cxb5+- Nikcevic-
Vuksanovic, Heraklio 1993.

**8 bxc3 ♘xc3 9 ♕c2 ♗xf3 10
gxf3 ♕g5+ 11 ♔h1 ♕h5 12 ♖g1!**
A superb move which sacrifices
another pawn to maintain the initiative. The players could also make an
early peace agreement after 12 ♔g2
♕g5+ 13 ♔h1 ♕h5 14 ♔g2 ♕g5+.

12 ... ♕xf3+ 13 ♖g2 f5
Black is struggling in other lines:

a) 13 ... ♕xd1+ 14 ♕xd1 ♘xd1
15 ♗c2 ♘c3 16 ♗b2+-.

b) 13 ... d5 14 ♗a3 ♘e4 15 cxd5
exd5 16 ♗xe4 ♕xe4 17 ♕xc7 ♘d7
18 ♖c1 f5 19 ♕d6+- (Nunn).

after 7 0-0

after 11 ... ♕h5

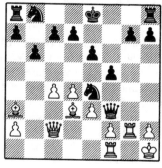

after 15 ♖f1

14 ♗a3

A precautionary measure to stop Spassky castling kingside. The obvious 14 ♕xc3 fails after 14 ... ♕d1+ 15 ♔g1 ♕f3+ 16 ♖g2 ♕d1+ and the game again ends in perpetual check.

14 ... ♘e4 15 ♖f1 ♖g8?!

15 ... ♘c6 is the best bet but after 16 d5 ♘e5 17 ♗e2 White has the more promising future.

16 ♗e2 ♕h3 17 f3 ♘f6 18 d5 ♔f7

An admission that something has gone wrong. Spassky would prefer to sort out his retarded development but 18 ... ♘a6 walks into 19 dxe6! ♘ac5 (19 ... dxe6 20 ♕a4+ wins) 20 ♗xc5 bxc5 21 exd7+ ♔d8 22 ♖d1+-.

19 e4 c5 20 ♗b2 f4 21 e5

White continues to gain space on the board and now finds an ingenious way to trap the black queen.

21 ... ♘h5

There is no relief in 21 ... ♘e8 which is well met by 22 ♕e4.

22 ♔g1 g6 23 ♖g4

Introducing the threat of 24 ♖f2 and 25 ♗f1.

23 ... ♖d8 24 ♗d3

A subtle shuffle threatening ♗xg6+ and cornering the queen under the most favourable circumstances.

24 ... ♖g8 25 ♖f2 1-0

Since 25 ... ♘g7 26 ♗xg6+ hxg6 27 ♕xg6+ ♔e7 28 ♕f6+ ♔e8 29 ♖xg7 ♖xg7+ 30 ♕xg7 ♕f5 31 dxe6 ♕xe6 32 ♕h8+ ♔e7 33 ♖g2 leaves White completely winning according to an analysis by Nunn.

after 18 d5

after 21 e5

after 25 ♖f2

Torre Attack: 4 c3
Hebden-Grabuzova
Cappelle la Grande 1997

1 d4 e6 2 ♘f3 ♘f6 3 ♗g5 c5 4 c3
A speciality of Hebden who prefers to avoid the well known lines associated with 4 e3.

4 ... cxd4 5 cxd4 h6
Alternatives are:

a) 5 ... ♕a5+ 6 ♘bd2 ♗e7 7 e3 h6 8 ♗h4 ♘c6 9 a3 a6 10 ♗d3 d5 11 0-0 b5 12 ♘e5 ♘xe5 13 dxe5 ♘d7 14 ♗xe7 ♔xe7 15 f4 ♗b7 16 ♘f3 g6 17 ♘d4+= Horvath-Sziebert, Budapest 1995.

b) 5 ... ♕b6 6 ♕b3 (6 ♕c2!?) 6 ... ♘e4 7 ♗f4 ♘c6 8 e3 ♗b4+ 9 ♘bd2? g5! 10 ♗xg5 ♗xd2+ 11 ♘xd2 ♕a5 0-1 Sangla-Karpov, USSR Team Championship 1968.

6 ♗xf6 ♕xf6 7 e4
It makes sense to seize the centre but the dull 7 e3 has been tried in the past.

7 ... ♗b4+ 8 ♘c3 0-0 9 ♖c1 ♕g6 10 ♗d3
The threat of e5 encourages Black to be greedy.

10 ... ♕xg2 11 ♖g1 ♕h3 12 a3 ♗xc3+ 13 ♖xc3
In return for the pawn White has a lead in development and a half-open g-file, already occupied by a strong rook. Moreover the black queen is running out of decent squares.

13 ... b6 14 ♘e5 ♕h4 15 ♗b1 ♘c6 16 ♖cg3
Hebden goes straight for the kill with simple chess.

16 ... ♘xe5
Or 16 ... g5 is well met by 17 ♘f3! ♕f4 18 ♘xg5+-.

17 ♖xg7+ ♔h8 18 dxe5 ♗a6 19 ♕f3 ♖ac8 20 ♖1g4 1-0

after 4 c3

after 10 ♗d3

after 16 ♖cg3

Dutch: Leningrad 5 ♗g5
Smyslov-Beliavsky
Sochi 1986

1 d4 f5 2 c4 ♘f6 3 ♘c3 g6 4 ♗g5 ♗g7 5 ♕d2

An innocuous-looking move but one which has caught out a number of good players. The idea is to meet the obvious 5 ... 0-0 by 6 ♗h6 d6 7 ♘f3 c6 8 h4 with a strong attack.

5 ... c5

Other moves are: a) 5 ... h6 6 ♗xf6 exf6 7 e3 ♘c6 8 d5 ♘e5 9 f4 ♘f7 10 ♗d3 h5 11 ♘f3 d6 12 ♘h4 ♖h6 13 0-0-0 ♗d7 14 ♖he1 and the threat of e4 leaves Black's king dangerously vulnerable, Miles-Wockenfuss, Bad Lauterberg 1977.

b) 5 ... ♘c6 6 0-0-0 h6 7 ♗xf6 ♗xf6 8 e4 ♘xd4 9 exf5 gxf5 10 ♘ge2 c5 11 ♘xd4 cxd4 12 ♘b5 ♕b6 13 ♘xd4 0-0 14 h4 d6 15 ♖h3 ♗d7 16 ♕xh6 ♗g7 17 ♖g3 and White pushed his h-pawn to victory, Sadler-Tseitlin, Hastings 1991.

6 dxc5 ♘a6 7 ♗h6 ♗xh6 8 ♕xh6 ♘xc5 9 ♘h3?!

This plan of pursuing the h-pawn via g5 is rather slow. Smyslov should prefer 9 f3 ♕a5 10 0-0-0 b5 11 cxb5 a6 12 e4! with double-edged play according to Beliavsky.

9 ... ♕a5 10 0-0-0 b5 11 ♘g5 ♗b7 12 ♕g7

The ex-World Champion is chasing the h-pawn but at the neglect of getting his kingside pieces into play.

12 ... ♖f8 13 ♘xh7 ♘xh7 14 ♕xh7 b4 15 ♘d5 ♗xd5 16 ♖xd5 d6 17 ♔b1 b3! 18 axb3 ♖b8

White's undeveloped kingside cannot help the defence and Beliavsky is ready to pounce.

19 ♕xg6+ ♔d7 20 ♖xf5 ♕e1+ 21 ♔c2 ♘xb3 0-1

after 5 ♕d2

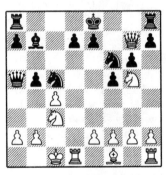

after 12 ♕g7

after 21 ... ♘xb3

Spanish: Worrall Attack 6 ♕e2
Posazennikov-Lane
Leuven 1995

1 e4 e5 2 ♘f3 ♘c6 3 ♗b5 a6 4 ♗a4 ♘f6 5 0-0 ♗e7 6 ♕e2

This way of playing the Spanish is a favourite of mine which makes it doubly difficult for my opponent to play against!

6 ... b5

A small percentage of players fall into the mire with 6 ... 0-0, allowing 7 ♗xc6 dxc6 8 ♘xe5 ♕d4 9 ♘f3 ♕xe4 10 ♕xe4 ♘xe4 11 ♖e1+-.

7 ♗b3 0-0 8 c3 d5 9 d3

9 exd5 is a critical alternative but concedes the initiative, so it is not surprising that Black came out better in the game Calzetta-Mitkov, Las Palmas 1995: 9 ... e4 10 ♘g5 (10 dxc6 ♗g4!) 10 ... ♘a5 11 ♗c2 ♗g4 12 f3 exf3 13 ♘xf3 ♖e8 14 d4 ♕xd5 15 ♕d3 ♗h5 16 ♘e5 ♗g6 17 ♘xg6 hxg6 18 ♗f4 c5=+.

9 ... ♗b7 10 ♖d1

Against Michael Adams, London 1993, I tried 10 ♘bd2 which apparently made him confuse his systems. The game continued 10 ... ♖e8 11 a3 ♗f8 12 ♖e1 ♘b8? 13 exd5 ♘xd5 14 d4 ♘c6 15 dxe5 ♘f4 16 ♕e4 and White eventually won.

10 ... ♖e8 11 ♗g5 ♘a5 12 ♘xe5

This looks good but I soon regain the pawn with the bonus of a powerful pair of bishops.

12 ... ♘xb3 13 axb3 dxe4 14 dxe4 ♗d6 15 ♘g4 ♗xe4 16 ♘xf6+ gxf6 17 ♗e3 f5 18 f3 ♗b7 19 ♕d3 ♕h4! 20 ♘d2

20 g3 is destroyed by 20 ... ♗xg3-+.

20 ... ♗xh2+ 21 ♔f1 ♖ad8 0-1

after 6 ♕e2

after 11 ... ♘a5

after 19 ... ♕h4

Queen's Gambit Accepted: 3 ... a6
Illescas-Anand
2nd Match Game, Leon 1997

1 d4 d5 2 c4 dxc4 3 ♘f3 a6 4 e3
White chooses to transpose to the Classical variation. Other tries:

a) 4 a4!? ♘c6 5 ♘c3 ♘a5 6 ♗f4 ♘f6 7 e4 e6 8 ♕c2 ♗b4 9 ♖d1 b5 10 ♗e2 ♗b7 11 0-0 0-0 and Black held on to the extra pawn, Garcia-Dlugy, New York 1991.

b) 4 e4 b5 5 a4 ♗b7 6 b3 e6 7 bxc4 bxc4 8 ♘c3 ♗b4 9 ♗d2 ♘f6 10 e5 ♘d5 11 ♕c1 ♘xc3 12 ♗xc3 c5 13 dxc5 ♕a5 14 ♗xb4 ♕xb4+ 15 ♘d2 ♕xc5 16 ♘xc4 0-0 17 ♕e3 ♕xe3+ 18 ♘xe3 ♘d7 gave Black a pleasant ending in Ivanov-Salov, St Petersburg 1997.

4 ... ♘f6 5 ♗xc4 e6 6 0-0 c5 7 ♗b3 ♘c6 8 ♕e2 cxd4 9 ♖d1 ♗e7 10 exd4 ♘a5! 11 ♗c2 b5 12 ♘c3 ♗b7 13 ♘e5 ♖c8 14 a3 0-0 15 ♖d3 ♘c4! 16 ♖g3?

White offers a pawn in exchange for pressure on the g-file; Anand suggests that 16 ♗g5 ♘d5 is equal.

16 ... ♕xd4! 17 ♗h6
Consistent, since if 17 ♘xc4 ♖xc4 Black is better.

17 ... ♘xe5
It seems risky to accept the material in the face of an attack but there are always exceptions to the rule.

18 ♖xg7+
Or 18 ♖d1 and now ... ♕c5 19 ♗xg7 ♘g6 blunts the onslaught.

18 ... ♔h8 19 ♖d1
The pin on the knight with 19 ♖g5 can be refuted by 19 ... ♖g8! 20 ♖xe5 ♖xg2+ 21 ♔f1 ♘g4-+.

19 ... ♕c5 20 ♖d5
Great vision but it is flawed.

20 ... ♗xd5 21 ♕xe5 ♗e4! 0-1

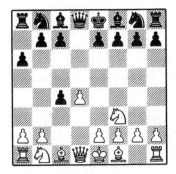

after 3 ... a6

after 9 ♖d1

after 16 ♖g3

Conclusion

The pros and cons of accepting material have to be carefully considered. Snatching even a single pawn in the opening can be perilous if it leaves your development in a backward state. Though pawn-grabbers sometimes have the last laugh, more common is the fate of Smyslov against Beliavsky where the ex-world champion's excursion to win pawns ends in disaster after his defenceless king falls victim to a violent counter-attack.

Another warning is sounded by the game Hebden-Grabuzova. Here Black's win of a hot pawn merely leads to the opening of a line of attack against his own king, thus enabling the opponent to break through in double-quick time.

The Art of Attack

1 You can sacrifice material to gain a lead in development.

2 Remember that long-term pressure can be sufficient compensation for material loss.

3 Promote your attack with an aggressive piece formation and do not think that your opponent will automatically lose just because his queen is spending time capturing every available pawn.

The Art of Defence

1 Think before you capture material. There is usually some motive behind a sacrifice.

2 Calculate accurately. There are many cases where material is wildly sacrificed only for the subsequent attack to be abruptly rebuffed by a strong defensive move.

3 Do not lag behind in development. A great many defeats can be attributed to neglect of this basic general principle. Sometimes winning a pawn is simply not worth all the trouble!

2 Chasing the King

The king-hunt is one of the most spectacular ways of gaining victory and is sure to provide you with lasting happy memories—unless, of course, you happen to be on the losing side! It is surprising how often the right conditions for a king hunt arise but also how often chances are missed.

The king is usually well fortified behind a row of pawns and can only be prised open by means of a sacrifice. Once on an open board, however, the poor monarch will find itself subject to attack by hostile pieces and running for its life in a fruitless attempt to avoid checkmate. Nevertheless such a sacrifice entails a degree of risk since it often involves the precise calculation of many variations. Here it is often necessary to trust your intuition.

Our illustrative games show the power of such factors as better development and accurate calculation and the role these play in the chase.

Though it may sound as if we can all win the brilliancy prize, opportunities still have to be spotted —as well as blind alleys. In the games Movsziszian-Stoll, Short-Piket and Shaked-Raptis the king is dragged into the open yet ends up perfectly safe! A study of such games will add a note of caution before you next invest material on a king hunt.

One great advantage of chasing a king in the opening is that the opponent's pieces will probably not have had time to get coordinated and may even still be sitting on their original squares—as is the case in Romero Holmes-Soto Perez.

A final reminder that amazing games are not confined to the modern era is the classic attack Lasker-Thomas, a personal favourite of mine.

In this chapter we have gone further than give examples of pure tactical calculation and attempted to explore the very foundations of a successful king hunt.

Austrian Attack: 7 e5
Hansen-Hoi
Danish Championship 1998

1 e4 g6 2 d4 ♗g7 3 ♘c3 d6 4 f4 ♘f6 5 ♘f3 0-0 6 ♗d3 ♘bd7 7 e5

The usual line with 7 0-0 can be answered with 7 ... e5 8 fxe5 dxe5 9 d5 c6 10 dxc6 bxc6 11 ♔h1 which gives White a slight advantage.

7 ... ♘e8 8 ♘g5!

A critical move which telegraphs White's aggressive intentions.

8 ... dxe5

a) 8 ... h6? 9 ♘xf7! ♔xf7 10 e6+ ♔xe6? 11 ♕g4+ ♔f7 12 ♗c4+ d5 13 ♗xd5+ ♔f6 14 ♘e4 mate.

b) 8 ... e6?! 9 h4 h6 10 h5 hxg5 11 hxg6 fxg6 12 ♗xg6 ♖xf4 13 ♗xf4 gxf4 14 ♕h5 ♔f8 15 0-0-0 ♕e7 16 ♖hf1 dxe5 17 dxe5 ♘xe5 18 ♖xf4+ ♘f6 19 ♕xe5 wins Flogaus-Hahnewald, Bundesliga 1988.

c) 8 ... ♘b6 (recommended by Nunn who assesses the position as unclear) 9 ♗e3 c6 10 h4 f6? 11 ♘xh7! f5 (11 ... ♔xh7 12 ♕h5+ ♔g8 13 ♗xg6+-) 12 h5 ♔xh7 13 hxg6+ ♔g8 14 ♕h5 ♘f6 15 exf6 ♖xf6 16 ♕h7+ ♔f8 17 ♕h8+ 1-0 Ankerst-Ramseier, Silvaplana 1993.

9 fxe5 ♘b6 10 ♗e3 c6 11 0-0 ♘c7 12 ♘xh7! ♘bd5

Fireworks follow 12 ... ♔xh7, e.g. 13 ♖xf7! ♖xf7 14 ♕h5+ ♔g8 15 ♗xg6 ♗e6 16 ♕h7+ ♔f8 17 ♗h6 ♔e8 18 ♕xg7 ♕xd4+ 19 ♔h1 ♕f2 20 ♖d1 ♘cd5 21 ♘e4 winning.

13 ♘xd5 ♘xd5 14 ♗g5 ♔xh7 15 ♖xf7 ♖xf7 16 ♕h5+ ♔g8 17 ♗xg6 ♘f4 18 ♗xf7+ ♔f8 19 ♕h7!

Intending ♖f1.

19 ... ♕xd4+ 20 ♔h1 ♔xf7 21 ♖f1 ♕xe5 22 ♖xf4+ ♔e8 23 ♕g6+ ♔d8 24 ♖e4 ♕d5 25 ♖xe7 1-0

after 7 e5

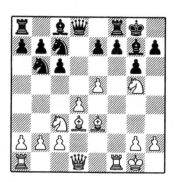

after 11...♘c7

after 19 ♕h7

French Tarrasch: 8 ... f6
Shaked-Raptis
Los Angeles 1991

1 e4 e6 2 d4 d5 3 ♘d2 ♘f6 4 e5 ♘fd7 5 ♗d3 c5 6 c3 ♘c6 7 ♘e2 ♕b6 8 ♘f3 f6

A common inaccuracy which is rarely punished. Black's idea is to avoid releasing the central tension as occurs in the normal continuation 8 ... cxd4 9 cxd4 f6.

9 exf6 ♘xf6 10 0-0 ♗d6

If Black tries to transpose into the main line with 10 ... cxd4 then White can play the surprising 11 ♘exd4 with pressure against e6, e.g. 11 ... ♗c5 12 b4! ♗xd4 13 cxd4 0-0 (13 ... ♘xb4 14 ♖b1 ♕d6 15 ♗a3 a5 16 ♕a4+ ♗d7 17 ♗xb4±) 14 b5 ♘e7 15 a4 intending ♗a3 which gives White excellent chances.

11 dxc5! ♗xc5 12 b4 ♗d6

The speculative sacrifice 12 ... ♗xf2+?!, seen in Van Baarle-Van Rijn, Dieren 1997, failed to a tactical sequence after 13 ♖xf2 ♘g4 14 ♘ed4 ♘xf2 15 ♔xf2 e5 16 ♘xe5! ♘xe5 17 ♕h5+ ♘g6 18 ♕xd5 ♖f8+ 19 ♔g1 ♖f7 20 ♗g5 ♗d7 21 ♖e1+ ♔f8 22 ♗c4 1-0

13 a3 ♘e5 14 ♘xe5 ♗xe5 15 ♗e3 ♕d8 16 ♗d4

Shaked enjoys a lead in development which prompts his opponent to take desperate measures.

16 ... ♗xh2+ 17 ♔xh2 ♘g4+ 18 ♔g3!

18 ♔g1 is met by 18 ... ♕h4 but now Black has problems cornering White's wandering king.

18 ... h5 19 ♗g6+ ♔e7 20 f4 e5 21 ♗c5+ ♔e6 22 f5+ ♔f6 23 ♕d2 b6 24 ♔h4 1-0

Superb! The king supports the threat of 25 ♕g5 mate.

after 8 ... f6

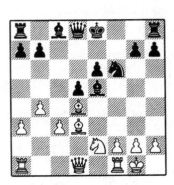

after 16 ♗d4

after 24 ♔h4

King's Gambit, Cunningham Defence
Short-Piket
Madrid 1997

1 e4 e5 2 f4 exf4 3 ♘f3 ♗e7 4 ♘c3 ♗h4+ 5 ♔e2

This line was popular over 100 years ago but has been unfashionable ever since and is very rarely seen at international level.

5 ... d5

The most direct, offering a pawn for quicker development. Others:

a) 5 ... c6 6 d4 d5 7 ♗xf4 ♗g4 8 ♕d3 ♘e7 9 g3 ♘g6 10 ♗xb8 ♖xb8 11 ♔f2 ♗f6 12 exd5 0-0 13 ♗g2 cxd5 14 ♖he1= David-Hebden, Isle of Man 1997.

b) 5 ... d6 6 d4 ♗g4 7 ♗xf4 ♘e7 8 ♕d3 ♘g6 9 ♗e3 0-0 10 ♔d2 ♗xf3 11 gxf3 ♗g5 12 ♗xg5 ♕xg5+ 13 ♕e3 ♕xe3+ ½-½ Olesen-Lukacs, Budapest 1994.

6 ♘xd5 ♘f6 7 ♘xf6+ ♕xf6 8 d4 ♗g4 9 ♕d2!

A clever improvement on moves such as 9 c3 and 9 e5. Short intends to shelter the king by ♔d1-c2.

9 ... ♘c6 10 c3 0-0-0!? 11 ♕xf4 ♕e6 12 ♔e3 g5 13 ♘xg5 ♗xg5 14 ♕xg5 f5 15 h3!

A crucial move as 15 ♗d3 is well met by 15 ... ♘xd4! 16 cxd4 ♕b6 when the onslaught continues.

15 ... ♘xd4 16 cxd4 ♖xd4 17 hxg4

White could even get away with snatching the rook, e.g. 17 ♔xd4 ♕xe4+ 18 ♔c3 ♕e5+ 19 ♔c2 ♕e4+ 20 ♗d3 ♕xg2+ 21 ♗d2 ♕c6+ 22 ♗c3 winning.

17 ... ♖xe4+ 18 ♔f2 fxg4 19 ♖h6 ♖f8+ 20 ♔g1 ♖xf1+ 21 ♔xf1 ♖e1+ 22 ♔f2 ♕e2+ 23 ♔g3 ♕d3+ 24 ♔xg4 1-0

after 5 ♔e2

after 9 ♕d2

after 16 ... ♖xd4

French: Classical Variation
Topalov-Bareev
Linares 1994

1 e4 e6 2 d4 d5 3 ♘c3 ♘f6 4 ♗g5 dxe4

Avoiding the mass of theory associated with 4 ... ♗b4 and 4 ... ♗e7.

5 ♘xe4 ♗e7 6 ♗xf6 ♗xf6 7 c3 ♘d7 8 ♕c2

An old idea recommended by the theory books. If Black castles next move, White can build-up a reasonable attack by f4, 0-0-0, ♗d3 and ♘f3.

8 ... e5!

after 8 ♕c2

Bareev seizes the initiative. In the game Weenink-Maroczy, Holland 1930, White gained the better ending after 8 ... ♕e7 9 0-0-0 0-0 10 f4 c5 11 g4 g6 12 g5 ♗g7 13 ♘f3 cxd4 14 ♘xd4 e5 15 fxe5 ♕xe5 16 ♗g2 ♘c5 17 h4 ♘xe4 18 ♕xe4 ♕c5 19 ♕d5.

9 dxe5 ♘xe5 10 f4 ♘g6 11 g3 0-0 12 ♗d3 ♕d5!

White was intending 13 0-0-0+=.

13 a3?!

13 ♘e2 should be considered.

13 ... ♘xf4! 14 ♘xf6+

14 gxf4 is bad, e.g. 14 ... ♗h4+ 15 ♔f1 (15 ♔d2 ♖d8 or 15 ♔e2 ♗g4+ 16 ♘f3 f5-+) 15 ... f5 16 ♘f3 fxe4 17 ♗xe4 ♗h3+ 18 ♔g1 ♕c5+ 19 ♘d4 ♖xf4-+.

14 ... gxf6 15 ♗xh7+ ♔g7 16 ♕e4 ♖e8! 17 ♕xe8 ♗f5!!

after 17 ... ♗f5

In 19th century romantic style, Black sheds another piece in name of the attack. The white queen will be diverted from its defensive role.

18 ♕xa8 ♕e4+ 19 ♔f2 ♕g2+ 20 ♔e3 ♘d5+ 21 ♔d4 ♕d2+

The brilliancy prize is assured!

22 ♔c5 ♕e3+ 23 ♔c4 ♘b6+ 0-1

after 21 ... ♕d2+

English: 3 ... f5
Seirawan-Browne
Berkley 1979

**1 c4 e5 2 ♘c3 ♘c6 3 ♘f3 f5 4 d4
e4 5 ♘g5 h6 6 ♘h3 g5**
Browne boldly advances on the
kingside in an attempt to exploit the
time wasted by White's king's
knight.
7 f3

after 6 ... g5

a) 7 e3 ♘f6 8 ♘g1 d6 9 h4 ♖g8
10 hxg5 hxg5 11 f3 exf3 12 ♘xf3
♗d7 13 d5 ♘e5 14 ♗e2 ♕e7 15
♘xe5 ♕xe5 16 ♕d4 ♕g3+ with the
initiative, Lindenmaier-Ikonnikov,
Germany 1995.

b) 7 ♘g1 ♘f6 8 h4! g4 9 e3 ♘h5!
10 ♘ge2 ♘e7 11 ♗d2 ♗g7 12 ♕b3
d6 13 ♘d5 ♘g6= Polugaevsky
-Seirawan, Haninge 1990.

7 ... exf3 8 exf3 ♗g7 9 d5?!
9 ♗e3 is better.

9 ... ♕e7+ 10 ♔d2!?
This is quite ambitious but under-
standable in view 10 ♕e2 ♕xe2+ 11
♗xe2 ♘d4 when Black's strong
dark-squared bishop gives him a
comfortable ending.

10 ... ♘d4 11 ♗d3 ♔d8!
A remarkable position has arisen
with both players having moved
their kings to the d-file. In Black's
case it was to avoid the pin by ♖e1.

after 11 ... ♔d8

**12 ♘g1 b5 13 ♘ge2 bxc4 14
♗xc4 ♕c5 15 ♔d3?!**
Or 15 b3 ♗a6 16 ♗xa6 ♘xe2 17
♔xe2 ♕xc3 18 ♖b1 ♕a5 19 ♗d3
♕xd5∓.

**15 ... ♖b8 16 ♗e3 ♕xc4+! 17
♔xc4 ♗a6+ 18 ♘b5 ♘xb5 0-1**
In view of 19 ♔d3 ♘c3+ 20 ♔c2
♖xb2+ 21 ♔xb2 ♘xd1+ 22 ♔c1
♘xe3-+ or 19 ♘d4 ♘d4+ 20 ♔c3
♘e2+ 21 ♔d2 ♖xb2+ 22 ♔e1 ♗c3+
23 ♔f2 ♘f4+ 24 ♔g1 ♖xg2 mate.

after 16 ♗e3

Catalan: 7 ♕a4
Korniushin-Kofanov
Novgorod 1997

1 d4 d5 2 ♘f3 e6 3 g3 ♘f6 4 ♗g2 c5 5 0-0 ♘c6 6 c4 dxc4 7 ♕a4

The Catalan has the reputation of being solid but White can create complications with this pin on the knight.

7 ... ♗d7 8 ♕xc4 cxd4 9 ♘xd4 ♖c8 10 ♘c3 ♗e7

10 ... ♘xd4 11 ♕xd4 ♗c5 12 ♕h4 ♗c6 13 ♖d1 ♕b6 14 ♗c6+ ♖xc6 (14 ... ♕xc6 15 ♗h6!) 15 ♗h6! ♗f8 (15 ... ♗xf2+ 16 ♔g2 0-0 17 ♗xg7 ♔xg7 18 ♕g5+ ♔h8 19 ♕xf6+ and 20 ♕xf2) 16 ♖d2 a6 17 ♖ad1 ♖c8 18 e4 ♖c8 19 e5! ♘g8 20 ♗g5 ♘e7 21 ♕a4+ ♘c6 22 ♘e4 h6 23 ♗f6 ♖g8 24 a3 ♗e7 25 ♗xe7 ♔xe7 26 ♕c4 1-0 Hulak-Sahovic, Nis 1985.

11 ♖d1 ♕b6?! 12 ♘xc6 ♗xc6 13 ♗e3 ♕xb2?! 14 ♖ab1 ♕a3

14 ... ♕c2!? gives White fewer attacking options but this does not necessarily make Black's position any more palatable after 15 ♗xc6+ bxc6 (15 ... ♖xc6? 16 ♕xc6+ bxc6 17 ♖b8+ ♗d8 18 ♖bxd8+ ♔e7 19 ♗c5 mate) 16 ♗xa7+=.

15 ♗xc6+ ♖xc6

15 ... bxc6 16 ♘b5! ♕a7 17 ♘a7+-.

16 ♕xc6+!

A worthy finishing touch to a splendid game.

16 ... bxc6 17 ♖b8+ ♗d8 18 ♖dxd8+ ♔e7 19 ♖xh8 ♕xc3 20 ♖b7+ ♔d6

The king is forced towards the centre of the board. 20 ... ♘d7 can be met by 21 ♖a8!+-.

21 ♖d8+ ♔e5 22 ♗d4+ ♕xd4 23 ♖xd4 ♔xd4 24 e3+ 1-0

after 7 ♕a4

after 15 ... ♖xc6

after 20 ♖b7+

Dutch: 2 g4
Movsziszian-Stoll
Bad Wörishofen 1997

1 d4 f5 2 g4!?
To divert the f-pawn and take over the centre.

2 ... fxg4
The only way to test this outlandish sacrifice is to accept it. In Herlemann-Sauer, Baden, 1992, 2 ... e6 3 gxf5 exf5 4 e4! d5 (4 ... fxe4? 5 ♕h5+ g6 6 ♕e5+ wins) 5 e5 ♗e6 6 ♘h3 ♗e7 7 ♖g1 ♔f8 8 ♘c3 c5 9 ♘f4 ♕d7 10 dxc5 d4 11 ♕xd4! was clearly good for White.

3 e4 d5
a) 3 ... e5 4 dxe5 ♘c6 5 ♕xg4 (5 ♗f4!? ♕e7 6 ♘c3! maintains the tension) 5 ... d6 6 ♕g5 ♕xg5 7 ♗xg5 ♘xe5= Kozlovskaya-Prudnikova, Rjazan 1992.

b) 3 ... d6 4 ♗d3 ♘c6 5 h3 ♘f6 6 hxg4 ♗xg4 7 f3 ♗d7 8 e5 dxe5 9 ♖xh7! 1-0 Heldele-Fliter, Deizisau 1998.

4 e5 ♗f5 5 ♘e2! ♕d7 6 ♘g3 ♘c6?!
Preferable is 6 ... e6.

7 c3 g6
7 ... 0-0-0 8 h3 h5 (8 ... gxh3? 9 ♘xf5 ♕xf5 10 ♗xh3+-) 9 ♘xf5 ♕xf5 10 ♗d3 ♕f3 11 ♕xf3 gxf3 12 ♗f5+ ♔b8 13 ♘d2 allows White to regain his pawn with a superior ending.

8 h3 gxh3 9 ♘xf5 ♕xf5 10 ♘d2! ♗h6 11 ♗xh3! ♗xd2+ 12 ♔xd2 ♕xf2+ 13 ♔d3 ♕g3+ 14 ♗e3
Though White's king is exposed Black's attack is too lightweight.

14 ... ♘xe5+ 15 dxe5 ♕xe5 16 ♕a4+ ♔f7
16 ... c6 17 ♗f4±.

17 ♖af1+ ♘f6 18 ♖xf6+! ♕xf6 19 ♖f1 1-0

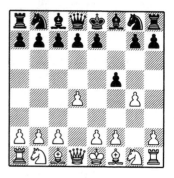

after 2 g4

after 7 c3

after 14 ♗e3

Bishop's Opening: 2 ... d6
Krakops-Meijers
Riga 1998

1 e4 e5 2 ♗c4

As early as move two White can
dictate the style of play. White now
has options of transposing to other
lines, according to how Black responds. Another bonus is that, un-
like the move-order 2 ♘f3 ♘c6 3
♗c4, this system avoids the need to
learn how to combat the Petroff.

2 ... d6

After 2 ... ♘f6 I can personally
recommend 3 d3.

a) 3 ... c6 4 ♘f3 d5 5 ♗b3! ♗d6
(5 ... dxe4 6 ♘g5!+=) 6 ♘c3 ♗e6 7
♗g5 ♕a5 8 0-0 ♘bd7 9 ♖e1 0-0-0
10 d4 exd4 11 ♘xd4 ♗g4 12 ♕d2
dxe4 13 ♘xe4 ♗c7 14 ♘d6+! ♔b8
15 ♘xf7 h6 16 ♗f4 1-0 Lane-
Pergericht, Brussels 1990.

b) 3 ... ♘c6 4 ♘f3 ♗c5 5 c3 d6 6
0-0 0-0 7 ♗b3 a6 8 ♘bd2 ♗a7 9 h3
h6 10 ♖e1 ♘h5 11 ♘f1 ♕f6 12
♗e3 ♗e6 13 ♗xa7 ♖xa7 14 ♘e3
♘f4 15 ♔h2 ♖aa8 16 ♘g1 g5 17
♖f1 ♖ad8 18 g3 ♘g6 19 ♕h5 ♔h7
20 ♘f3 ♗xb3 21 axb3 ♖h8 22 ♘d5
♕g7 23 ♘xg5+ ♔g8 24 ♘f3 1-0
Lane-Timmermans, Amsterdam
1998.

3 d4 exd4 4 c3 dxc3?!

Allowing White to develop quickly. 4 ... ♘f6 is better.

**5 ♘xc3 ♘d7 6 ♘f3 ♘b6 7 ♗b3
♗e7 8 a4 ♘f6 9 a5 ♘bd7 10
♗xf7+!**

Devastating Black's position.

10 ... ♔xf7 11 ♘g5+ ♔g6

11 ... ♔e8/♔g8 12 ♕b3+ wins.

12 f4

Simple but effective.

**12 ... ♘e5 13 f5+ ♗xf5 14 exf5+
♔xf5 15 ♕c2+ 1-0**

after 2 ♗c4

after 9 ♘bd7

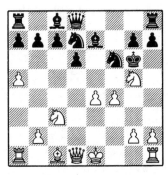

after 12 f4

Sicilian Four Knights: 4 ♗b5
Romero Holmes-Soto Perez
Malaga 1998

1 e4 c5 2 ♘f3 ♘f6 3 ♘c3
Avoiding the complications of 3
e5 ♘d5 4 ♘c3 e6 5 ♘e4 f5.
3 ... ♘c6 4 ♗b5
This is a good way to continue
against a player waiting to transpose
to the Sveshnikov system after 4 d4
cxd4 5 ♘xd4 e5. The game position
can also arise after 1 e4 c5 2 ♘c3
♘c6 3 ♘f3 ♘c6 4 ♗b5.
4 ... ♘d4
To avoid White's capture on c6,
doubling the pawns.
**5 e5 ♘xb5 6 ♘xb5 ♘d5 7 ♘g5
h6?**
A typical mistake inviting a king
hunt. Though older sources assume
the position is roughly equal, recent
developments put White on top, e.g.
a) 7 ... ♘c7 8 ♕h5 g6 9 ♕f3 f5 10
exf6 d6 11 ♘xc7+ ♕xc7 12 0-0
♗h6 13 d4 ♗xg5 14 ♗xg5 h6 15
♗h4 ♕c6 16 f7+ ♔f8 17 ♗xe7+
1-0 Yakovich-Reinderman, Leeuwarden 1994.
b) 7 ... e6 8 ♘e4 ♕h4 9 ♕f3 f5 10
exf6 gxf6 11 g3 1-0 Kovalev-Klees-
chaetzky, Berlin 1994.
**8 ♘xf7 ♔xf7 9 ♕f3+ ♔e6 10 c4
♘b6**
10 ... ♘b4 11 a3 ♘c2+ 12 ♔d1
♘xa1 13 g4! and 14 ♕f5 decides.
11 d4 d5
11 ... d6 is not much of an improvement after 12 d5+ ♘xd5 (12 ...
♔d7 13 e6+ ♔e8 14 ♕f7 mate) 13
cxd5+ ♔xe5 14 b4! and the queen's
bishop will stylishly deliver mate.
**12 dxc5 ♘xc4 13 ♘d4+ ♔d7 14
e6+ ♔c7 15 ♗f4+ 1-0**

after 4 ♗b5

after 7 ... h6

after 11 d4

Sicilian Dragon: Yugoslav Attack
Ziatdinov-Sehner
Dieren 1990

1 e4 c5 2 ♘f3 d6 3 d4 cxd4 4 ♘xd4 ♘f6 5 ♘c3 g6 6 ♗e3 ♗g7 7 f3 ♘c6 8 ♕d2 0-0 9 0-0-0

The Yugoslav Attack is White's main weapon against the Dragon.

9 ... ♘xd4 10 ♗xd4 ♗e6 11 ♘d5

Avoiding the theoretical 11 ♔b1.

11 ... ♗xd5

White has all the fun after 11 ... ♘xd5 12 exd5 ♗d7 13 ♗xg7 ♔xg7 14 h4.

12 exd5 a6?!

There is no time to waste in such a cut-throat line. Other possibilities:

a) 12 ... ♕c7 13 ♔b1 (the direct attack with 13 h4 has a big drawback after 13 ... ♖fc8 14 h5 ♗h6!-+)
13 ... ♖fc8 14 c3 ♕a5 15 c4 ♕xd2 16 ♖xd2 ♘d7 17 ♗e2+= Dvoirys-Stisis, Groningen 1994.

b) 12 ... ♘d7 13 ♗xg7 ♔xg7 14 h4 ♘f6 15 h5 ♖c8 16 hxg6 fxg6 17 g4 ♖c5 18 ♕h6+ ♔g8 19 g5 ♕c7 (19 ..♘h5 20 ♖xh5! gxh5 21 g6+-) 20 ♗h3 ♖xc2+ 21 ♔b1 ♖e2 22 ♗e6+ ♖xe6 23 gxf6 exf6 24 dxe6 1-0 Luther-Danner, Budapest 1991

13 h4! ♕c7 14 h5 ♖ac8 15 ♗d3 ♘xd5

After 15 ... ♘xh5 16 ♗xg7 ♔xg7 17 g4 ♘f6 18 ♕h6+ ♔g8 19 g5 ♘h5 20 ♖xh5 wins.

16 ♗xg7 ♔xg7 17 hxg6 hxg6 18 ♗e4 ♘b6 19 ♕h6+ ♔f6 20 ♖h5!

Cutting off the king's escape.

20 ... e6

Or 20 ... e5 21 ♕g5+ ♔e6 22 ♗xg6 fxg6 23 ♕xg6+ ♖f6 24 ♕g4+ ♔e7 25 ♖h7+ wins.

21 ♕g5+ ♔g7 22 ♖h7+! 1-0

Black is mated after 22 ... ♔xh7 23 ♕f6 followed by ♖h1-h8.

after 9 0-0-0

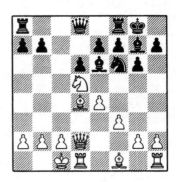

after 11 ♘d5

after 20 ♖h5

Dutch: 2 ♘c3
Ed.Lasker-Thomas
London 1912

1 d4 f5 2 ♘c3 ♘f6 3 ♘f3 e6 4 ♗g5 ♗e7 5 ♗xf6 ♗xf6 6 e4 fxe4 7 ♘xe4 b6

Or 7 ... d5 8 ♘xf6+ ♕xf6 9 c3 ♘d7 10 ♕d2 0-0 11 ♕e3 ♕h6 12 ♕xh6 gxh6 13 ♗e2 a6 14 0-0 c5 15 ♖fe1 b6 16 ♗d3 ♖f6 17 ♖e3 ♖a7 18 g3 ♖c7 19 ♖ae1 ♖f7 20 ♘h4 ♘f8 21 f4, Korchnoi-Meulders, Brussels 1987, with a better ending.

8 ♘e5

The preference nowadays is for the less committal attacking build-up by 8 ♗d3. For instance: 8 ... ♗b7 9 ♕e2 ♕e7 10 0-0-0 ♘c6 11 c3 0-0-0 12 ♗a6 g6 13 ♖he1 ♖hf8 14 ♕b5 ♗xa6 15 ♕xa6+ ♔b8 16 d5 ♘a5 17 d6 cxd6 18 ♘xd6 ♔a8 19 b4 ♖b8 20 bxa5 bxa5 21 ♕xa5 ♖b6 22 ♕a3 ♖c8 23 ♕xa7+! 1-0 Bisguier-Burtman, USA 1995.

8 ... 0-0 9 ♗d3 ♗b7 10 ♕h5 ♕e7?

10 ... ♗xe5 gives Black a reasonable game but he assumes that 11 ♘xf6+ gxf6 will allow the queen to guard h7. Sir George Thomas' talents extended also to the tennis court where he reached the last eight at Wimbledon. Then, in 1923, he achieved the distinction of becoming British Champion at both badminton and chess. Remarkable, but such is chess trivia that he is probably best remembered for allowing the following combination!

11 ♕xh7+! ♔xh7 12 ♘xf6+ ♔h6

12 ... ♔h8 13 ♘g6 mate.

13 ♘eg4+ ♔g5 14 h4+ ♔f4

Black has no choice.

15 g3+ ♔f3 16 ♗e2+ ♔g2 17 ♖h2+ ♔g1 18 ♔d2 mate.

after 4 ♗g5

after 10 ... ♕e7

after 18 ♔d2 mate

Conclusion

This feast of glorious king-hunts should be an inspiration to everyone.

Some openings offer more chances of creating a strong attack than others. In the Dragon Sicilian game, Ziatdinov-Sehner, it was all down to the player landing the first punch that determined whether it was the white or black king that had to walk the plank.

Nevertheless, opportunities for attack arise in all openings, even the solid French Defence which, in Topalov-Bareev, served as a spring-board for a vicious assault with a clever mating net—all arising from Black's better development.

At the very start of the game the weakest point in Black's position is the f7 pawn, defended only by the king. This was emphasised in Krakops-Meijers where White prospered by an initial sacrifice on f7 to oust the king from its camp.

The Art of Attack

1 You often need to sacrifice to expose the enemy king to attack.

2 Back up your attack with major pieces. Short-Piket shows that even if a king occupies a central square the attacker cannot break through without the strong initiative generated by heavy fire-power.

3 When chasing the king try to short-cut the calculation of myriads of variations by giving priority to forcing moves such as checks and captures. Also look for ways to cut off the king's escape and then go for checkmate.

The Art of Defence

1 In the opening try to castle early so your king is not easily attacked.

2 Do not be tempted by gain of material if this leaves your pieces sitting on their original squares. This happened in the game Movsziszian-Stoll where, as a result, the king came under a devastating attack.

3 Stay alert at all times. In Korniushin-Kofanov White even gave up his queen to chase the king and mate it with minor pieces.

3 Attacking the King in the Centre

The three golden rules of the opening are to develop your pieces, control the centre and safeguard your king by castling. However, rules are made to be broken and sheltering the king at an early stage is often forgotten in this modern era of razor-sharp opening theory.

Such neglect of king safety can occur for various reasons. For instance through fear of opposite-side castling, as in the game Seirawan-Ivanchuk where the threat of an attack on the kingside deters Black from castling. White's reaction is to open the centre to get at the king, even though he is not yet castled himself! Indeed, castling is not essential before launching an attack, especially if the co-ordination of the attacker's pieces is superior.

A player who sticks faithfully to pet lines can soon get into trouble if these opening variations run counter to basic chess principles, as in the game Wolff-Wall where Black voluntarily weakens his own position and the opponent's pieces come flooding in after a single sacrifice.

The attacking player will do all he can to stop the opposing king seeking shelter. This can be done by sacrificing or even subtle manoeuvring, as in Liardet-Kogan. The art of successfully attacking a king in the centre lies in judging the right moment to launch the assault.

All the games in this chapter have the common theme of creating and maintaining the initiative. The odd pawn is dropped here and there but a pattern soon emerges of superior development making its presence felt. Indeed the defender may fall further behind in development as repeated threats must be fended off, giving little or no time for mobilisation of barracked forces.

Therefore, it is worth remembering the importance of the co-ordination of your pieces. An advantage in space may not be very significant if your pieces lack harmony. On the other hand, in Schmaltz-Karpatchev Black has *all* the trumps—full and harmonious co-operation of his pieces, a space advantage and tactical threats directed against the white king stuck in the centre.

Basically, a king left in the centre is bad for three reasons:

1 It undermines the activity of the pieces because of the difficulty of getting the rooks into play. This allows the opponent to take a lead in development.

2 It is not safe. In particular the f2/f7 pawn is vulnerable because it is only defended by the king.

3 It is easier for the opponent to create direct attacks against the king when the centre is open.

Dutch Defence: 3 ♗g5
Atalik-Thang Trang
Budapest 1998

1 d4 f5 2 ♘f3 ♘f6 3 ♗g5 ♘e4 4 ♗f4 d6 5 ♘bd2 ♘xd2 6 ♕xd2 e6 7 e4!

With this enterprising sacrifice, the Turkish grandmaster follows one of the key principles of attacking an uncastled king—open lines in the centre!

7 ... fxe4 8 ♘g5 d5 9 f3 exf3 10 ♗d3 fxg2 11 ♕xg2

after 7 e4

This case is an extreme example of what can happen when you allow your pieces to hang about on their original squares. After just eleven moves it is clear that White has succeeded in demonstrating two out of three reasons why an uncastled king is such a liability. He has four pieces developed compared to Black's none and the centre has been successfully opened allowing for more channels of attack.

11 ... ♘c6 12 0-0 ♘e7 13 ♘f7! 1-0

Now it is three out of three reasons because the weakness of the king defending the f7 square has been exposed. 13 ... ♔xf7 14 ♗xc7+ wins.

after 11 ♕xg2

after 13 ♘f7

King's Indian Defence: 5 &d3
Seirawan-Ivanchuk
Groningen FIDE World Ch. 1997

1 d4 ♘f6 2 c4 g6 3 ♘c3 ♗g7 4 e4 d6 5 ♗d3

Seirawan has long been a champion of this move which steers clear of the main lines of the King's Indian and keeps options open on further development, depending on Black's response. There are similarities to the Samisch in that White can support the e-pawn with f3 while Black, for his part, will try to create active play by attacking the weakened d4 pawn.

5 ... e5

After 5 ... 0-0 6 ♘ge2 play can continue:

a) 6 ... a6 7 0-0 ♘bd7 8 f3 c6 9 ♗g5 b5 10 ♔h1 ♘b6 11 b3 bxc4 12 bxc4 ♘fd7 13 f4 c5 14 d5 f6 15 ♗h4 g5 16 ♗g3 ♕e8 17 ♖b1 ♖b8 18 ♖b3 ♘a8 19 ♖xb8 ♘xb8 20 ♕b1 ♘d7 21 e5! gxf4 22 ♗xh7+ ♔h8 23 ♗g6 ♕d8 24 ♕f5 ♗h6 25 ♗xf4 1-0 Christiansen-Babula, Bundesliga 1995.

b) 6 ... ♘bd7 7 ♗c2 a6 8 a4 e5 9 d5 a5 10 h3 ♘c5 11 ♗e3 ♘fd7 12 0-0 ♘a6 13 ♘a2 ♘dc5 14 ♕d2 ♗d7 15 ♕xa5 ♘xe4 16 ♕e1 ♘f6 17 b4 ♘h5 18 f3 f5 19 ♖b1 b6 20 ♘ac3 ♗f6 21 ♕d2 ♗h4 22 f4 ♗f6 ½-½ Seirawan-Ivanchuk, Reykjavik 1991.

6 d5 a5 7 ♘ge2 ♘a6 8 f3!?

Apparently after their game in Reykjavik (see the previous note) Seirawan actually recommended this move to his opponent! It turned out Ivanchuk dismissed it on the grounds that Black could exchange the dark-squared bishops then exert pressure on the queenside. They

after 5 ♗d3

after 8 f3

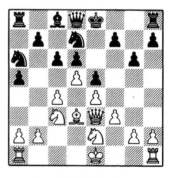

after 11 ... c6

disagreed about the merits of the plan: "this stuck in my craw ... so I thought I would test my judgement against his" commented the American.

8 ... ♘d7 9 ♗e3 ♗h6 10 ♕d2 ♗xe3 11 ♕xe3 c6?!

11 ... 0-0 looks logical but without the bishop on g7 the dark squares around the king look weak—the first indication that White's opening strategy has been a triumph.

12 ♕h6 ♘dc5 13 ♖d1 ♕b6 14 ♗b1 ♔e7

An admission that his king will now be well and truly stuck in the centre, but he has few options. After 14 ... ♕xb2 15 dxc6 bxc6 16 ♖xd6 the alternatives 17 ♕g7 or 17 ♖xc6 leave Black in a mess. It is important to note that, although White has not castled, he can still activate his rooks. Black, on the other hand, is in no position to form any significant counterplay against the roller coaster attack.

15 f4 exf4 16 ♖f1 ♖f8 17 ♕xf4

White's forces are piling in against the hapless black king and something has to give.

17 ... f6 18 dxc6 ♕xc6 19 ♘d4 ♕e8 20 ♘d5+ ♔d8 21 ♕xd6+ ♗d7 22 ♘b5 1-0

Black resigned in view of the various threats such as 23 ♕b6+ ♔c8 24 ♘d6+ or simply 23 ♘bc7.

after 11...c6

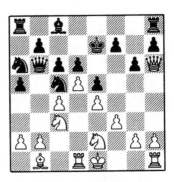

after 14 ... ♔e7

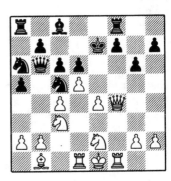

after 17 ♕xf4

French Winawer: 5 ♗d2
Watson-Hurley
Kilkenny 1997

1 e4 e6 2 d4 d5 3 ♘c3 ♗b4 4 e5 c5 5 ♗d2

A relatively unusual continuation enabling White to recapture on c3 with the bishop after ... ♗xc3. Over-analysed lines are avoided and Black is set critical problems at a very early stage of the opening.

5 ... ♗d7?!

In the game Lutz-Costello, Ostend 1992, Black tried 5 ... cxd4 and went astray in the complications after 6 ♘b5 ♗f8 (6 ... ♗xd2+ 7 ♕xd2 intending ♘d6+ is in White's favour) 7 ♘f3 ♘c6 8 ♘bxd4 f6?! (8 ... ♘ge7!?) 9 ♗b5 ♗d7 10 0-0 fxe5 11 ♗xc6 bxc6 12 ♘xe5 c5 13 ♕h5+! g6 14 ♕f3 ♕f6 15 ♘xd7 ♔xd7 16 ♕b3 ♖c8 17 ♕a4+ ♔d8 18 ♗g5! 1-0

6 dxc5! ♗xc5 7 ♕g4

Now 7 ... ♗f8 looks like a record-breaking attempt to return all the pieces to their original squares while 7 ... ♔f8 gives up the right to castle.

7 ... g6 8 ♘f3 ♕b6 9 0-0-0 ♗xf2 10 ♗d3

Watson has shed a pawn to activate his pieces aggressively.

10 ... ♗e3 11 ♖hf1 ♘h6 12 ♕h3 ♔f8 13 ♘g5!

Black's position is so full of holes it resembles Swiss cheese.

13 ... ♗xd2+ 14 ♖xd2 ♔g7 15 ♖df2 ♗e8 16 ♖f4 ♕d8 17 ♖f6 ♘d7 18 ♕xe6!

Bravo!

18 ... ♘xf6

18 ... fxe6 19 ♘xe6+ ♔g8 20 ♖f8+ ♘xf8 21 ♖xf8 mate.

19 exf6+ ♔g8 20 ♕h3 ♘f5 21 ♖xf5 1-0

after 5 ♗d2

after 10 ♗d3

after 18 ♕xe6

Nimzo-Indian: 4 f3
Liardet-Kogan
Geneva 1998

**1 d4 ♘f6 2 c4 e6 3 ♘c3 ♗b4 4 f3
d5 5 a3 ♗d6**

Black rejects the standard moves
5 ... ♗c3 or 5 ... ♗e7 in favour of a
provocative manoeuvre. The idea is
to entice White to create a pawn
centre—incidentally threatening a
pawn fork on e5—and then later
smash it down!

6 e4 c5 7 cxd5 exd5 8 ♗b5+

The game Halldorsson-Barle,
Reykjavik 1988, continued 8 e5
cxd4 9 ♕xd4 ♘c6 10 ♗b5 ♕e7! 11
♗f4 0-0 12 ♗xc6 ♗c5 13 ♘xd5
♘xd5 14 ♕xd5 ♖d8 15 ♕b3 bxc6
16 ♘e2 ♗a6 (echoing our main
game as Black has devastating control of the g1-a7 diagonal) 17 ♖d1
♖xd1+ 18 ♕xd1 ♖d8 19 ♕c1 ♗b6
20 h4 ♕e6 21 ♖h3 ♕b3 22 g4 ♕d3
23 ♕d2 ♕c4 24 b3 ♕xb3 25 ♕c1
♕d3 26 ♖h2 ♕xf3 0-1

**8 ... ♗d7 9 ♗xd7+ ♘bxd7 10
dxc5 ♗xc5 11 ♘xd5 ♘xd5 12
♕xd5 ♕b6**

White has won a pawn but Black
controls the g1-a7 diagonal thereby
preventing kingside castling.

**13 ♘h3 ♖d8 14 ♘f4 0-0 15 ♔e2
♘e5**

At one stroke Kogan opens the
d-file for the queen's rook and adds
the knight to the attack. 16 ♕xe5
loses the queen after 16 ... ♕b5+ 18
♔e1 ♗f2+.

**16 ♕a2 ♕b5+ 17 ♔e1 ♘d3+ 18
♘xd3 ♕xd3 0-1**

Since 19 ♗f4 ♗e3 is crushing.

after 5 ... ♗d6

after 12 ... ♕b6

after 15 ... ♘e5

Scotch: 4 ... ♕h4
Schmaltz-Karpatchev
Cappelle la Grande 1993

1 e4 e5 2 ♘f3 ♘c6 3 d4 exd4 4 ♘xd4 ♕h4

The most aggressive Black defence against the Scotch. Having played it myself I know it has tremendous surprise value.

5 ♘c3

It is easy for White to go wrong:

a) 5 ♕d3?! ♗c5 6 c3 ♘f6 7 ♘d2 ♘g4 8 g3 ♕f6 9 f3 ♗xd4 10 cxd4 ♘b4 11 ♕c3 ♘e3 12 ♔f2 ♘d1+ 0-1 Nunez- Ferron, Abierto 1994;

b) 5 ♗e2?! ♗c5 6 c3 ♕xe4 7 ♘xc6 ♕xg2 0-1 Neubauer-Hresc, St.Veit 1995;

c) 5 ♗e3 ♕xe4 6 ♘d2 ♕e7 7 ♗e2 ♘f6 8 0-0 ♘d5 9 ♘f5 ♘xe3 10 fxe3 ♕c5 11 ♘e4 ♕e5 12 ♘c3 g6 13 ♘g3 ♗g7 left Black a pawn up in Tyehimba-Post, Philadelphia 1992;

d) 5 ♘b5 ♗c5 6 ♕e2 ♘d4 7 ♘xd4 ♗xd4 8 c3 ♗b6 9 g3 ♕e7 10 ♗g2 d6 11 ♗e3 ♘f6 12 ♘d2 0-0 13 0-0 ♖e8= Schuermans-Lane, Le Touquet 1991.

5 ... ♗b4 6 ♘db5 ♗a5 7 ♗d3 a6 8 ♘a3 b5 9 ♗d2 ♘f6 10 g3 ♕h3 11 ♘d5 ♘xd5 12 exd5 0-0

Inspired chess! By activating his king's rook, Black aims to take advantage of the exposed white king

13 dxc6 ♖e8+ 14 ♗e2 dxc6 15 ♖f1

If 15 ♗xa5 then 15 ... ♗g4 is good for Black.

15 ... ♗g4 16 f3 ♕xh2 17 ♗xa5 ♖ad8 18 ♗d2 ♕xg3+ 19 ♖f2 ♗h3 0-1

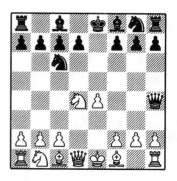

after 4 ... ♕h4

after 12 ... 0-0

after 19 ... ♗h3

Sicilian c3: 5 ... ♗g4
Nisipeanu-Moldovan
Bucharest 1997

1 e4 c5 2 ♘f3 ♘c6 3 c3 d5 4 exd5 ♕xd5 5 d4 ♗g4 6 ♗e2 e6 7 h3 ♗h5 8 c4

Much better than the normal 8 ♗e3 because White intends to exploit Black's undeveloped king's knight to force through d4-d5.

8 ... ♕d8?!

8 ... ♕d6 also allows White to create an attack. Keitlinghaus-Fogarasi, Budapest 1996 continued 9 d5!? ♗xf3 10 ♗xf3 ♘d4 11 dxe6 ♕xe6+ 12 ♗e3 ♕xc4 13 ♗xd4 cxd4 (13 ... ♕xd4 14 ♕e2+ ♗e7 15 ♘c3 gives White a strong initiative) 14 ♘d2 ♕b5 15 a4 ♕a6 16 ♕b3 0-0-0? (16 ... ♕e6+ 17 ♕xe6+ fxe6 18 ♗xb7 ♖b8=) 17 ♖c1+ ♔b8 18 ♖c6! b6 19 ♕xf7 ♗d6 20 ♖xd6 ♖xd6 21 ♕f8+ ♔c7 22 ♕xg7+ 1-0.

9 d5 ♗xf3 10 ♗xf3 exd5

The difference between 8 ... ♕d8 and 8 ... ♕d6 is revealed. Now, after 10 ... ♘d4 11 dxe6, the queen cannot take back on e6.

11 ♗xd5 ♘ge7 12 ♘c3 ♘xd5 13 cxd5 ♘d4 14 ♗e3 ♘f5 15 ♕a4+ ♕d7 16 ♕e4+ ♔d8

The king has to move because 16 ... ♗e7 is well met by 17 ♗xc5.

17 d6! ♘xe3 18 fxe3 ♖c8 19 ♕h4+ f6 20 0-0-0 ♖c6

20 ... ♗xd6? fails completely to 21 ♘e4 ♖c6 22 ♘xd6 ♖xd6 23 ♕g3+-.

21 ♖d5 ♖xd6? 22 ♖hd1 ♔c7 23 ♕g3 1-0 Black resigned due to 23 ... ♔c6 24 ♖xd6 ♗xd6 25 ♕f3+ ♔c7 26 ♘e4 and the bishop is lost.

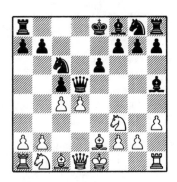

after 8 c4

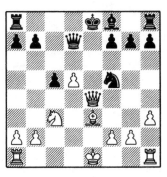

after 16 ♕e4+

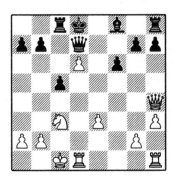

after 20 0-0-0

Reti: 3 b4
Benjamin-Brookshear
New York 1990

1 ♘f3 d5 2 c4 d4 3 b4

White states his aggressive intentions after only three moves. He intends to attack the d4 pawn and wishes to deter ... c5.

3 ... f6

To support ... e5. Others:

a) 3 ... g6 4 e3 dxe3 5 fxe3 ♗g7 6 d4 ♘f6 7 ♘c3 0-0 8 ♗e2 ♗g4 9 0-0 c6 10 h3 ♗xf3 11 ♗xf3 ♘bd7 12 b5 cxb5 13 ♘xb5 with good play against b7, Fridman-Mattheus, Hamburg 1997.

b) 3 ... ♗g4 4 ♕b3 f6 5 e3 dxe3 6 dxe3 e5 7 c5 ♘c6 8 ♘c3 a5 9 ♗c4 (the power of the a2-g8 diagonal is a theme also explored in the main game) 9 ... ♘h6 10 b5 a4 11 ♕c2 ♘a5 12 ♗d3 ♗xc5 13 0-0 ♕d7 14 ♘xa4 and White had a clear advantage in Nikcevic-Todorovic, Cetinje 1992.

c) 3 ... a5 4 b5 c5 5 e3 g6 6 exd4 cxd4 7 d3 ♗g7 8 g3 when White has the better chances due to the weakness of the d4 pawn.

4 e3 dxe3 5 fxe3 e5 6 c5 e4 7 ♘d4 ♘c6 8 ♘xc6 bxc6 9 ♗c4

Whites cuts out the possibility of Black castling kingside.

9 ... ♘h6 10 0-0 ♕e7 11 ♘c3 g6 12 ♗b2 ♗g7 13 ♘xe4 ♕xe4 14 ♖f4 ♕e7 15 ♕f3

The sacrifice has paid off. The twin threats of 16 ♕xc6+ and 16 ♖e4 are winners.

15 ... ♕f8 16 ♖e4+ ♔d8 17 ♖d4+ 1-0

after 3 b4

after 9 ♗c4

after 15 ♕f3

Grob Defence 1 ... g5
Wolff-Wall
London 1985

1 e4 g5?!

Michael Basman has thought up a number of weird and wonderful openings and this is one of them. But, once he has recovered from shock, White can perhaps undermine the weakened kingside.

2 d4 h6 3 ♘c3

In Ginsburg-Basman, London 1979, White tried 3 c4 preferring to dominate the centre with his pawns. There followed 3 ... d6 4 ♘c3 ♘c6 5 h4 gxh4 6 d5 ♘e5 7 f4 ♘g6 8 ♘f3 ♗g7 9 ♗d3 ♗g4 10 ♕a4+ ♔f8 11 ♘xh4 ♘xh4 12 ♖xh4 h5 13 ♖h1 c5 with a small advantage, although Black still won after 68 moves.

3 ... ♗g7 4 h4 gxh4 5 ♘f3 d6 6 ♘xh4 ♘c6 7 d5 ♘e5 8 ♗e2

Even in his youth the future American champion played in very mature style. While Black struggles to develop his pieces and get castled queenside, Wolff is busy activating his pieces

8 ... ♘f6 9 ♗f4 ♘eg4 10 ♘f5 ♗xf5 11 exf5 h5 12 ♗b5+ ♘d7 13 ♖xh5!

A nice sacrifice which forces Black to endure a passive position.

13 ... ♖xh5 14 ♕xg4 ♖h7 15 f6 exf6 16 ♔d2!

The king steps out of the way for the rook to check on the e-file. On the other hand 16 0-0-0 ♕e7! would have still allowed Black hopes of survival. After the text, however, even at this early stage Black has no decent moves.

16 ... f5 17 ♕xf5 ♖h4 18 g3 ♖h2 19 ♖e1+ ♔f8 20 ♗xd7 ♖xf2+ 21 ♔d1 1-0

after 1 ... g5

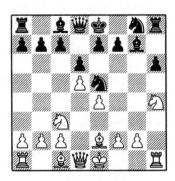

after 9 ♗e2

after 16 ♔d2

Vienna: 5 ♔e2
Gavrilov-Potapov
Russia Cup 1997

1 e4 e5 2 ♘c3 ♘c6 3 f4 exf4 4 d4
This astounding move was first played by Steinitz in 1867. The position can also arise from a King's Gambit after 1 e4 e5 2 f4 ♘c6 3 ♘c3 exf4 4 d4!?.

4 ... ♕h4+ 5 ♔e2
Though Steinitz claimed that the White king was in no real danger, being free to move to either flank, the modern view is that it gets in the way of the other pieces. Nevertheless Black has to be careful that his queen is not chased around the board.

5 ... b6 6 ♘b5 ♗a6 7 a4 0-0-0 8 ♘f3 ♕g4!?
The inspiration behind White's romantic choice of opening might be traced back to the game Martin-Adams, London 1992, which continued: 8 ... ♕e7 9 ♔f2 ♗b7 10 ♗xf4 ♕xe4 11 ♕d2 ♘f6 12 ♗d3 ♕d5 13 ♖he1 d6 14 a5 and White had the advantage. Even though Adams is a world class player, improvements were bound to be found as this game was played at a fast time-limit.

9 ♔f2 ♗b7 10 ♗d3 a6 11 ♘c3 ♘f6 12 ♖e1 g5 13 e5?
13 a5!? b5 14 ♘xb5 axb5 15 a6 ♗a8 16 ♗xb5 ♘a7 and Black fends off the attack.

13 ... ♘xd4! 14 ♗xa6
14 ♘xd4 ♕xg2 mate is embarrassing.

14 ... ♗xa6 15 ♘xd4
15 ♕xd4 ♗c5 wins.

15 ... ♕h4+ 16 ♔g1 ♘g4 17 h3 ♗c5 18 hxg4 ♗xd4+ 19 ♕xd4 ♕xe1+ 20 ♔h2 h5 0-1

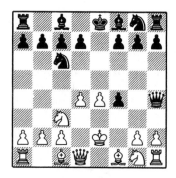

after 5 ♔e2

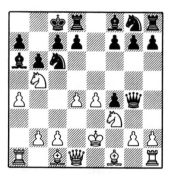

after 8 ... ♕g4

after 13 ... ♘xd4

Conclusion

In most of the games examined it is clear that the loser had played indifferently in the opening and suffered as a consequence.

Gavrilov-Potapov demonstrates the perils of blindly following theory especially when most of it was established over 100 years ago. It is a risky business ignoring such a basic principle as development of pieces. And there are better places for a king to seek shelter than on e2!

A choice of opening can be crucial as illustrated by the game Wolff-Wall where Black's offbeat opening moves were cruelly exploited. No wonder 1 ... g5 is no longer in Tim Wall's repertoire!

Atalik-Thang Trang is a short lesson on the perils of snatching material. All the Turkish grandmaster's pieces are directed against the opposing monarch with predictable consequences.

Always remember, as an attacker, your primary objective should be to deprive the opposing king of safety.

The Art of Attack

1 Exploit weak squares around the king, as in Benjamin-T.Brookshear.

2 Sacrifice to keep the king in the centre as in Schmaltz-Karpatchev.

3 Remember that the threat can be stronger than the execution. In the game, Seirawan-Ivanchuk, Black was so worried about castling into an attack that he left his king in the middle of the board where it proved to be even more vulnerable.

4 Take advantage of an opponent's lack of development, due to weak opening play, as seen in Wolff-Wall, Atalik-H.Thang Trang and Gavrilov-Potapov.

5 Disrupt the coordination of the opponent's pieces, as in the game Nisipeanu-Moldovan where a pawn was used to split the Black army into two, thereby creating a total lack of harmony.

In cases like these, where the defence tended to be rather poor, the attacking player had all the fun with bold attacks and scintillating sacrifices

The Art of Defence

1 Take preventive measures against any possible escalation of an enemy attack. As a general rule, the best antidote is to whisk the king to safety by castling early.

2 Go on the offensive if the opposing king is in the centre. In his game against Ivanchuk, Seirawan, after ruling out any possibility of enemy counterplay, went over to the attack even though his own king remained uncastled.

3 Choose tried and tested openings. If an opening is rarely played there is usually a good reason—reserve 1 ... g5 strictly as a surprise weapon!

4 Attacking the Castled King

Mastering the various techniques of attacking the castled position is of the greatest importance because these are among the most typical situations occurring in practical play. How often do we hear a player complain that he had obtained a good attacking position from the opening but failed to capitalise on it.

Prior to embarking on an attack, it is paramount to have some kind of positional superiority whether this be in the form of a space advantage, more effective development or better pawn structure. Any one of these factors can help to tip the balance and provide the impetus for an initiative. This applies both to same-side and opposite-side castling—although in the latter case, where both sides often indulge simultaneously in all-out attack, *timing* is absolutely critical.

Some opening systems allow the opponent to gain an early space advantage by setting up a big pawn centre—only to smash this later with blows from the flanks and follow up with a counterattack. However, the game Morozevich-Bratchenko, an Alekhine Defence, is a perfect example of what can happen if this plan goes wrong. White uses the extra space to improve the position of his pieces and quickly launch an attack.

The Open Sicilian invariably leads to a sharp game and Timman-Van Wely is no exception. White batters the defence with a weakness-probing pawn advance and then sacrifices material to expose the opponent's king. Kasparov-Kengis, another Sicilian, is more evidence of the effectiveness of this technique.

The demolition of the enemy pawn cover is a frequently recurring theme. The game Bacrot-Magem is another fine example and sees White firstly taking time to isolate the king from its defenders before going for a final attack.

If you have ever dreamed of playing a Hollywood star then take a look at the game Limbos versus Humphrey Bogart—not just of human interest but also a nice minature with an instructive finish.

Opposite-sides castling can lead to double-edged positions where everything depends on who holds the initiative. In Howell-Miles, White starts off with every intention of launching an all-out attack but this soon backfires with Black launching a powerful counter-offensive which slices through the opponent's vulnerable defences.

It is a different story in the game Gofshtein-Beikert where, due to the closed nature of the position, White has plenty of time to build up his forces in an orderly fashion before making a final, well-prepared assault.

The lesson is always to think positively. If you grab the initiative then you are on course for victory!

Sicilian Najdorf: 6 ... ♘c6
Timman-Van Wely
6th Match Game, Breda 1998

1 e4 c5 2 ♘f3 d6 3 d4 cxd4 4 ♘xd4 ♘f6 5 ♘c3 a6 6 ♗e3 ♘c6
The usual move here is 6 ... e5 but Van Wely prefers to try to transpose to a Scheveningen or English Attack.
7 h3
An odd-looking move but it prepares g4 with a position similar to a Keres Attack. In the second game in this match Timman tried 7 ♕e2 to facilitate queenside castling. Then followed 7 ... ♘xd4 8 ♗xd4 e5 9 ♗e3 ♗e6 10 f4 exf4 11 ♗xf4 ♖c8 and Black had equalised.
7 ... e6 8 g4 ♗e7 9 ♗g2 h6?!
This is a cautious approach because after 9 ♗g2 it is clear that White intends to castle kingside. In Borge-Rytshagov, Groningen 1997, Black whisked his king to safety with 9 ... 0-0. The game continued: 10 0-0 ♘xd4 11 ♕xd4 e5 12 ♕d2 ♗e6 13 ♔h1 ♖c8 14 a4 ♖c4 15 b3 ♖c8 16 ♖fc1 ♕c7=.
10 f4 ♕c7 11 0-0 ♘xd4 12 ♕xd4 e5 13 ♕d2 exf4 14 ♖xf4 ♗e6 15 ♖af1 0-0
In view of White's well placed pieces it is more prudent to try 15 ... ♘d7 but Timman has considerable pressure after 16 ♘d5 ♗xd5 17 ♕xd5.
16 ♖xf6! ♗xf6 17 ♖xf6 gxf6 18 ♕f2 ♔g7?
Or 18 ... ♕a5 19 ♗xh6 ♕c5! 20 ♗e3 maintaining White's chances, according to Timman.
19 e5 fxe5 20 ♗xh6+! ♔g6 21 ♕h4 1-0

after 6 ... ♘c6

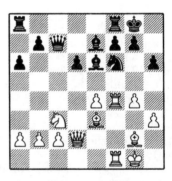

after 15 ... 0-0

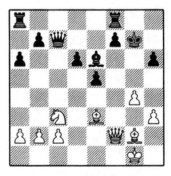

after 19 ... fxe5

Alekhine: Four Pawns
Morozevich-Bratchenko
Novgorod 1997

1 e4 ♘f6 2 e5 ♘d5 3 d4 d6 4 c4 ♘b6 5 f4 dxe5 6 fxe5 ♘c6

White has a space advantage but in the long-term Black hopes to undermine the pawns.

7 ♗e3 ♗f5 8 ♘c3 e6 9 ♘f3 ♗e7!?

A sharp continuation which invites Morozevich to enter wild complications.

10 d5 exd5 11 cxd5 ♘b4 12 ♘d4 ♗c8?!

This is unusual. Others:

a) 12 ... ♕d7?! 13 a3 ♘4xd5 (13 ... ♗g4 14 e6!+-) 14 ♘xd5 ♕xd5 (14 ... ♗h4+ 15 g3 ♕xd5 16 ♖g1 ♕xe5 17 ♘xf5±) 15 ♘xf5 ♕xe5 16 ♕f3+- Djurhuus-Egeli, Norwegian Championship 1998.

b) 12 ... ♗g6 13 ♗b5+ c6 14 dxc6 0-0 15 cxb7 ♖b8 16 0-0 ♖xb7 17 ♕f3+= Cheutshenko-Danilov, Tallinn 1998.

c) 12 ... ♗d7 (the best of the bunch) 13 e6 fxe6 14 dxe6 ♗c6 15 ♕g4 ♗h4+ 16 g3 ♗xh1 17 0-0-0 0-0 18 gxh4 ♕f6 19 ♗e2+= Texier-Solozhenkin, Noumea 1995.

13 ♗b5+ c6 14 dxc6 0-0 15 0-0 ♕c7 16 cxb7 ♗xb7 17 ♕g4 ♕xe5 18 ♖ae1 ♗d6 19 ♘f5!

This aggressive reaction caps a fine display.

19 ... ♗c8

If 19 ... ♕xh2+ then 20 ♔f2 g6 21 ♖h1 ♕xg2+ 22 ♕xg2 ♗xg2 23 ♘h6+ wins.

20 ♘h6+ ♔h8 21 ♕h4! ♗c5 22 ♘xf7+! 1-0

after 6 ... ♘c6

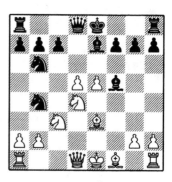

after 12 ♘d4

after 19 ♘f5

Grunfeld: Polugaevsky Variation
Polugaevsky-Kudrin
New York 1989

1 d4 ♘f6 2 c4 g6 3 ♘c3 d5 4 cxd5 ♘xd5 5 e4 ♘xc3 6 bxc3 ♗g7 7 ♗c4 c5 8 ♘e2 ♘c6 9 ♗e3 0-0 10 ♖c1

Heralding the Polugaevsky variation.

10 ... cxd4

The main line but Black has experimented with other replies:

a) 10 ... ♕c7 11 h4 ♖d8 12 h5 ♘a5 13 ♗d3 c4 14 ♗b1 e5 15 hxg6 hxg6 16 f4 ♗g4 17 fxe5 ♗xe5 18 ♕c2 ♗g7 19 ♘f4 ♖e8 20 ♕f2 ♕c6 21 e5 ♖ad8 22 ♕h4 f5 23 e6 1-0 Ward-Gillen, British Ch 1993.

b) 10 ... ♘a5 11 ♗d3 e5 12 dxe5 b6 13 f4 ♗e6 14 c4 ♕c8 15 ♕c2+= Krasenkov-Zezulkin, Polish Team Championship 1994.

11 cxd4 ♕a5+ 12 ♔f1 ♗d7 13 h4 ♖ac8

13 ... ♖fc8!? 14 h5 ♘d8 15 f3 gives White good chances.

14 h5 e5

A slight inaccuracy which leads to ruin because the position is so sharp. Polugaevsky suggested 14 ... e6 as an improvement but 15 hxg6 hxg6 16 e5! ♘e7 17 ♕d3 looks good for White.

15 hxg6 hxg6 16 d5! d4 17 ♘xd4 ♖xc4?

17 ... exd4 is essential although after 18 ♗d2! ♕b6 19 ♔g1 White has a strong centre.

18 ♖xc4 ♕a6 19 ♕d3! exd4 20 ♗xd4 ♗b5 21 ♕h3!

This is calculated brilliance.

21 ... ♗xc4+ 22 ♔g1 f6 23 ♕h7+ ♔f7 24 ♖h6! 1-0

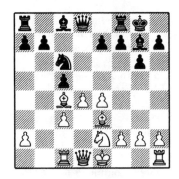

after 10 ♖c1

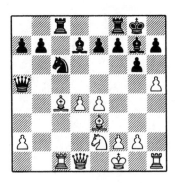

after 14 h5

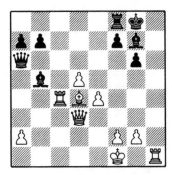

after 20 ... ♗b5

Nimzo-Indian: 5 ♕b3
Alterman-Kurajica
Dresden Zonal 1998

1 d4 ♘f6 2 c4 e6 3 ♘c3 ♗b4 4 ♘f3 b6 5 ♕b3 c5 6 ♗g5

This side-line is hardly known but deserves greater prominence. 6 a3 is more normal.

6 ... h6

Sokolov-Granda Zuniga, Wijk aan Zee 1997, continued 6 ... ♘c6 7 d5 ♘a5 8 ♕c2 h6 9 ♗h4 exd5 10 cxd5 0-0 11 e3 d6 12 ♗e2 ♗xc3+ 13 bxc3 ♕e7 14 ♘d2 ♗d7 15 0-0 ♖ae8 16 c4+=.

7 ♗h4 ♗b7

Alternatively:

a) 7 ... ♘c6 8 d5 ♘a5 9 ♕c2 ♘xc4 10 0-0-0 ♗xc3 11 ♕xc3 exd5 12 ♖xd5 ♘a5 13 ♖d6 ♕c7 14 ♖xf6!! as played in Miles-Kalesis, Chania 1997, was a great advert for the opening;

b) 7 ... g5 8 ♗g3 ♘e4 9 e3 ♗b7 10 ♗d3 ♗xc3+ 11 bxc3 ♘xg3 12 hxg3= Pachman-Muse, Baden Baden 1987.

8 e3 ♕e7 9 0-0-0

The scene is set for a kingside on-slaught by White. Black must look for chances in a queenside counter-attack. Timing is essential.

9 ... cxd4 10 exd4 ♗xc3 11 ♕xc3 d5 12 ♔b1 0-0 13 ♘e5 g5 14 ♗g3 dxc4 15 ♗xc4 ♖c8 16 h4!

Bravo! Alterman ignores the pin on the c-file and goes all out for the attack.

16 ... ♘d5

If 16 ... b5 then 17 hxg5 ♘e4 18 ♕e3 bxc4 19 g6! f6 20 ♕xh6 ♕g7 21 ♕xg7+ ♔xg7 22 ♖h7+ wins.

17 ♕d2 f6 18 hxg5 hxg5

Or 18 ... fxe5 19 ♖xh6 ♖xc4 20 ♗xe5+-.

19 ♗xd5 ♗xd5 20 ♖h8+ 1-0

after 6 ♗g5

after 9 0-0-0

after 15 ... ♖c8

Nimzowitsch Defence: 2 ... e5
Howell-Miles
Isle of Man 1995

1 e4 ♘c6 2 d4 e5 3 dxe5 ♘xe5
Miles is a specialist in this opening. The choice is perfect if Black wants to get his opponent into unfamiliar territory at an early stage of the game.
4 ♘c3
Others:
a) 4 f4 ♘c6 5 ♗c4 ♗b4+ 6 ♗d2 ♕h4+ 7 g3 ♕e7 8 ♕e2 ♗xd2+ 9 ♘xd2 d6 10 0-0-0 ♘f6 11 ♘gf3 0-0 12 h3 d5 13 exd5 ♕xe2 14 ♗xe2 ♘xd5 15 ♘c4 gave White a slight space advantage in Milov-Miles, Isle of Man 1995.

b) 4 ♘f3 ♘xf3+ 5 ♕xf3 ♕f6 6 ♕g3 ♕g6 7 ♕xc7 ♗d6 8 ♕c4 ♘f6 9 ♘c3 ♗e5 10 ♗d2 0-0 11 0-0-0 d5 12 exd5 b5 13 ♘xb5 ♗f5 14 ♗c3 ♖fc8 15 ♕a4 a6 16 ♘d4 ♖xc3! (the start of a brilliancy) 17 bxc3 ♖b8! 18 ♘b3 ♘e4 19 ♕xa6 ♕g5+ 20 ♔b2 ♘xc3 21 ♖e1 ♕d2 22 ♗d3 ♘e2+ 23 ♔b1 ♕c3 0-1 Hebden-Jadoul, Tarnby 1987.

4 ... ♗c5 5 ♗f4 d6 6 ♕d2 ♘f6 7 0-0-0 ♗e6 8 ♘a4 ♗b6 9 f3 0-0 10 a3 ♕e7 11 ♘xb6 axb6 12 ♘e2 ♘g6 13 ♔b1 d5!
An excellent way to open up the centre in order to activate the black pieces.
14 exd5
If 14 e5 Black can a win a pawn after 14 ... ♘d7 15 ♗g5 ♕e8.
14 ... ♘xd5 15 ♕c1 b5 16 ♗d2 b4 17 axb4 ♘xb4 18 b3 ♘xc2!
White's position now falls apart.
19 ♕xc2
Or 19 ♔xc2 ♖a2+ 20 ♔b1 ♖fa8 threatening ... ♖a1+ and ... ♗f5+ wins.
19 ... ♕a3 20 ♕c3 ♗xb3 0-1

after 3 ... ♘xe5

after 13 ♔b1

after 18 b3

Sicilian Taimanov: 6 ♗e2
Kasparov-Kengis
Riga 1995

1 e4 c5 2 ♘f3 e6 3 d4 cxd4 4 ♘xd4 ♘c6 5 ♘c3 ♕c7 6 ♗e2 a6 7 0-0

Black now has problems dealing with White's plan of simple development followed by an early f4 and a kingside attack.

7 ... ♘f6

a) 7 ... ♗c5 8 ♘b3 ♗e7 9 f4 b5 10 ♗e3 d6 11 ♗f3 ♘f6 12 e5 dxe5 13 fxe5 ♘d7 14 ♗xc6! ♕xc6 15 ♘a5 ♕c7 16 ♕f3+- Asrian-Fominyh, Minsk 1998.

b) 7 ... b5 8 ♘xc6 dxc6!? (8 ... ♕xc6 9 ♗f3 ♕c7 10 e5 ♗b7 11 ♗xb7 ♕xb7 12 f4+=) 9 ♗e3 ♗d6 10 f4 e5 11 ♕d2 exf4 12 ♗xf4 ♗xf4 13 ♖xf4 ♘e7 14 ♖af1= Rogic-Milov, Dresden Zonal 1998.

8 ♔h1 ♘xd4 9 ♕xd4 ♗c5 10 ♕d3 h5 11 ♗g5!?

A typical energetic move by Kasparov, in place of the usual 11 f4.

11 ... b5

If 11 ... ♘g4!? then White has excellent chances after 12 f4 ♘f2+ 13 ♖xf2 ♗xf2 14 e5 ♗c5 15 ♘e4.

12 f4 ♗b7 13 e5!? ♘d5 14 ♘xd5 ♗xd5 15 a4?!

15 ♗f3 would save a tempo.

15 ... ♕c6 16 ♗f3 ♗xf3 17 ♖xf3 bxa4 18 f5 ♖b8 19 ♖af1 0-0?

19 ... ♖xb2 is a marked improvement according to Kasparov: 20 fxe6 ♕xe6 21 ♖xf7 ♕xf7 22 ♖xf7 ♔xf7 23 h4 a3 24 ♕xd7+ ♔g8!=.

20 ♗f6!

A fantastic way to allow the rooks and queen to join in the attack.

20 ... ♕b5

20 ... gxf6 21 ♖g3+ ♔h8 22 ♕e2+-.

21 ♖g3 g6 22 ♕d1 exf5 23 ♖xf5 ♖b6 24 ♕xh5 1-0

after 7 0-0

after 11 ♗g5

after 19 ... 0-0

Queens's Gambit: 6 ♗g5
Bacrot-Magem
Pamplona 1997/98

1 d4 d5 2 ♘f3 ♘f6 3 c4 dxc4 4 ♘c3 e6 5 e4 ♗b4 6 ♗g5

The Vienna variation is renowned as an aggressive weapon for White.

6 ... c5

Black can also try:

a) 6 ... ♘bd7 7 ♗xc4 h6 8 ♗xf6 ♕xf6 9 0-0 0-0 10 a3 ♗xc3 11 bxc3 ♖d8 12 ♕e2 b6 13 a4 a6 14 ♘d2 ♗b7 15 f4+= Manor-Kosashvili, Rishon le Zion 1996.

b) 6 ... b5 7 e5 h6 8 ♗h4 g5 9 ♘xg5 hxg5 10 ♗xg5 ♘bd7 11 ♕f3 ♖b8 12 exf6 ♖g8 13 h4+= Lerner-Thesing, Berlin 1992.

7 ♗xc4 cxd4 8 ♘xd4 ♗xc3+

In the game Sokolov-Dizdar, Dresden Zonal 1998, Black refrained from exchanging pieces with 8 ... ♕a5 in order to preserve the tension. The game continued 9 ♗d2 ♕c5 10 ♗b5+ ♗d7 11 ♘b3 ♕e7 12 ♕e2 0-0 13 ♗d3 (13 e5) 13 ... e5 14 a3 ♗xc3 15 ♗xc3+=.

9 bxc3 ♕a5 10 ♘b5 0-0 11 ♗xf6 gxf6 12 ♕g4+ ♔h8 13 ♖d1!

The simple plan of ♖d3-h3 is a direct road to mate.

13 ... ♘d7 14 ♕h4 15 ♘d6 16 f4!

Bacrot takes time out to stop the black knight emerging via e5.

16 ... ♖g8

It is is difficult to organise a decent defence. After 16 ... ♘b6 White continues in a similar vein to the game with 17 e5! ♘xc4 18 ♘xc4 ♔g7 19 ♖d3+-.

17 0-0 ♘b6 18 ♖f3 ♘xc4 19 ♖h3 ♖g7 20 e5!

The final piece in the jigsaw.

20 ... ♘xd6 21 exf6 1-0

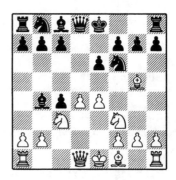

after 6 ♗g5

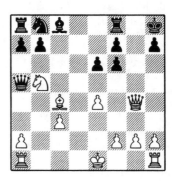

after 12 ... ♔h8

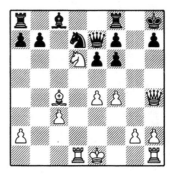

after 16 f4

Czech Benoni: 6 ... ♗g4
Gofshtein-Beikert
French Team Championship 1998

1 d4 ♘f6 2 c4 c5 3 d5 e5

The Czech Benoni is a solid response which avoids lots of theory. Unfortunately, Black's congested position is not to everybody's taste.

4 ♘c3 d6 5 e4 ♗e7 6 ♘f3 ♗g4

The white-squared bishop often ends up restricted in movement so Black is eager to exchange it. After 6 ... 0-0 7 h3 play might continue:

a) 7 ... a6 8 a4 ♘bd7 9 g4 ♘e8 10 ♗d3 h6 11 ♗e3 ♘c7 12 ♕d2 g5 13 h4+= Shirov-Lillo Ferrer, Villarrobledo rapidplay 1997.

b) 7 ... ♘e8 8 ♘f3 ♘a6 9 g4 ♘ac7 10 a3 ♗d7 11 b4 b6 12 ♖b1 ♖b8 13 ♗e3 left Black in a passive positon in Novikov-Alienkin, Rishon LeZion 1997.

7 h3 ♗xf3?!

It is probably better to preserve the bishop with 7 ... ♗h5. For example: 8 ♗d3 ♘a6 9 ♗e3 ♘c7 10 g4 ♗g6 11 ♕c2 a6 12 ♘e2 b5 13 b3 ♕b8 gives Black chances of a counter-attack.

8 ♕xf3 0-0 9 h4 ♔h8 10 g4

Game on! Gofshtein can safely advance his kingside pawns and continously improve his pieces.

10 ... ♘a6 11 ♗d2 ♘c7 12 g5 ♘g8 13 ♕g3 a6 14 a4 a5 15 f4 exf4 16 ♗xf4 f6 17 ♗e3 g6 18 0-0-0 ♖e8 19 ♗d3 ♘a6 20 e5!

Perfect timing. Now White can crash through on the kingside.

20 ... dxe5 21 h5 fxg5 22 hxg6 h6 23 ♘e4 ♔g7 24 ♘xg5 ♗xg5 25 ♗xg5 1-0

The lone rook mates after 25 ... ♕xg5+ 26 ♕xg5 hxg5 27 ♖h7+ ♔f8 28 ♖f7.

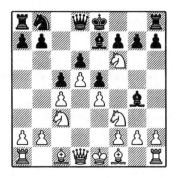

after 6 ... ♗g4

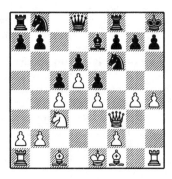

after 10 g4

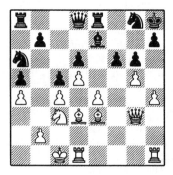

after 19 ... ♘a6

Caro-Kann: 5 ... exf6
Mnatsakanian-Simagin
Kiev 1965

1 e4 c6 2 ♘c3 d5 3 d4 dxe4 4 ♘xe4 ♘f6 5 ♘xf6+ exf6

This is no longer the height of fashion, perhaps because the game inevitably leads to a confrontation with opposite-sides castling.

6 ♗c4

after 6 ♗c4

Alternatives are:

a) 6 c3 ♗e7 7 ♗d3 ♗e6 8 ♘e2 0-0 9 ♕c2 g6 10 h4 f5 11 h5 ♖e8 12 ♘f4 ♗f6 13 ♔f1 ♘d7+= Kasparov-Miles, Israel 1998.

b) 6 g3 ♗d6 7 ♗g2 0-0 8 ♘f3 ♖e8+ 9 ♗e3 ♕a5+ 10 c3 ♕b5= Byrne-Bragg, Philadelphia 1991.

c) 6 ♘f3 ♗d6 7 ♗e2 0-0 8 0-0 ♖e8 9 ♗e3 ♘d7 10 ♕d2 ♕c7 11 c4 ♘f8 12 ♖fe1 ♗f5= Larsen-Hansen, Naestved 1988.

6 ... ♗e7

6 ... ♗d6 or 6 ... ♕e7 can also be considered but the text has a good record.

7 ♕h5

after 12 ... c4

In Gutierrez-Rahman, Dubai Olympiad 1986, White opted for a more restrained set-up with 7 ♘e2. The game continued: 7 ... 0-0 8 0-0 ♘d7 9 ♘g3 ♘b6 10 ♗d3 g6 11 ♖e1 ♗e6 12 c3 ♖e8+=.

7 ... 0-0 8 ♘e2 g6 9 ♕h6 ♗f5 10 ♗b3 c5 11 ♗e3 ♘c6 12 0-0-0 c4!

A crafty way of opening the c-file for Black's rook.

13 ♗xc4 ♘b4 14 ♗b3 ♖c8 15 ♘c3 ♕a5 16 ♔b1 ♖xc3!

The key defender leaves the board spelling doom and gloom for White.

17 bxc3 ♗xc2+ 0-1

There is no defence against 18 ♔c1 ♗xb3 18 axb3 ♕a2.

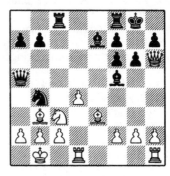

after 16 ♔b1

Closed Sicilian: 5 ♗e3
Ledger-Duncan
British League (4NCL) 1997

1 e4 c5 2 ♘c3 ♘c6 3 g3 g6 4 d3 ♗g7 5 ♗e3

A flexible move. White can aim for ♕d2 followed by ♗h6, to exchange bishops before advancing on the kingside, or quietly continue f4 with a solid position.

5 ... d6 6 ♕d2 e5

A critical junction:

a) 6 ... ♖b8 7 ♗g2 b5 8 ♘ge2 b4 9 ♘d1 ♘d4 10 0-0 e6 11 ♘c1 ♕a5 12 c3 bxc3 13 bxc3 ♘c6 14 ♗f4 ♕c7 15 ♘b3 e5 16 ♗g5 ♘ge7 17 ♗h6 0-0 18 ♗xg7 ♚xg7 19 f4 and White's slight advantage eventually led to a win in Ledger-Gallagher, British Championship 1997.

b) 6 ... e6 7 ♗g2 ♕a5 8 ♘ge2 ♘d4 9 0-0 ♘e7 10 ♚h1 ♗d7 11 f4 ♖b8 12 g4 h5 13 f5 ♗e5 14 fxg6 ♘xg6 15 g5 ♘xe2 16 ♕xe2 ♗xc3 17 bxc3 ♕xc3 18 ♕f2 ♕g7 19 d4 White had tremendous attacking chances in compensation for the pawn in Smyslov-Kottnauer, Moscow-Prague 1946.

7 f4 ♘ge7 8 ♗g2 0-0 9 ♘f3 ♖b8 10 0-0 exf4 11 ♗xf4 f5 12 ♗h6 b5 13 ♗xg7 ♚xg7 14 ♖ae1

The big difference is that Ledger's king is surrounded by pieces while Duncan's protective kingside cover is full of holes.

14 ... b4 15 ♘d5 fxe4 16 dxe4 ♗g4 17 ♘g5 ♕d7 18 ♘f6!

A touch of class.

18 ... ♖xf6

If 18 ... ♕c8 then 19 ♕xd6 ♖d8 20 ♘h5+! ♚h6 21 ♘f7+ ♚xh5 22 ♕f4 wins.

19 ♖xf6 ♚xf6 20 ♕f4+ ♗f5 21 exf5 ♕xf5 22 ♕xd6+ ♚g5 23 ♖f1 ♕xf1+ 24 ♚xf1 ♖b6 25 ♕f4+ 1-0

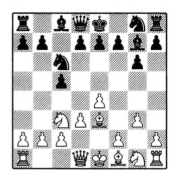

after 5 ♗e3

after 14 ♖ae1

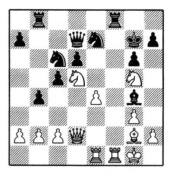

after 17 ... ♕d7

French Tarrasch: 3 ... ♘c6
Horvath-Kuligowski
Naleczow 1986

1 e4 e6 2 d4 d5 3 ♘d2 ♘c6 4 c3
A relative side-line compared to
the common 4 ♘gf3. For example
Lane-Cobb, British Championship
1998, continued 4 ... ♘f6 5 e5 ♘fd7
6 ♘b3 a5 7 a4 ♗e7 8 ♗b5+=.
**4 ... e5 5 exd5 ♕xd5 6 ♘gf3
exd4 7 ♗c4 ♕f5**
a) 7 ... ♕d8 8 cxd4 (8 0-0!?) 8 ...
♕e7+ 9 ♗e2 ♗e6 10 0-0+=
Micic-Gunawan, Belgrade 1988.
b) 7 ... ♕h5 8 cxd4 ♗e6 9 ♗xe6
(9 0-0!? 0-0-0 10 ♗e2 ♕d5 11 ♘b3
is a reasonable alternative for
White) 9 ... fxe6 10 ♕b3 0-0-0 11
0-0 ♘f6 12 ♕xe6+ ♔b8 13 ♘e4
♘xe4 14 ♕xe4 ♖e8 15 ♕d3 ♗d6
16 ♗d2 g5 17 g3 left Black with
compensation for the pawn in Xie
Jun-Brunner, Second Match Game,
Shanghai 1995.
**8 ♘xd4 ♘xd4 9 cxd4 ♗e6 10
♕a4+ ♗d7 11 ♕b3 0-0-0 12 0-0
♗e6 13 ♖e1 ♗xc4 14 ♘xc4 f6 15
♗e3 ♕d5 16 ♗f4 g5 17 ♗g3 ♘e7
18 ♖ac1 ♘c6 19 ♖e8!!**
A staggering move which de-
stroys Kuligowski's position.
19 ... ♕xd4
Or 19 ... ♖xe8 20 ♘b6+ cxb6 21
♕xd5±; 19 ... ♗e7 20 ♘b6+ axb6
21 ♕xd5±.
20 ♖xd8+ ♕xd8
Nothing can save Black. 20 ...
♘xd8 (20 ... ♔xd8 21 ♖d1+–) 21
♘b6+ ♕xb6 22 ♕xb6 axb6 23
♖xc7+ ♔b8 24 ♖c4+ ♔a7 25 ♖a4
mates.
21 ♘a5 ♗b4
The knight is taboo: 21 ... ♘xa5
22 ♕e6+ ♔b8 23 ♗xc7+ ♕xc7 24
♕e8+ ♕c8 25 ♖xc8 mate.
22 ♘xc6 ♕d2 23 ♕e6+ 1-0

after 4 c3

after 7 ♗c4

after 18 ... ♘c6

Spanish: Schliemann 4 ... ♘d4
Velicka-Souleidis
Gelsenkirchen 1998

1 e4 e5 2 ♘f3 ♘c6 3 ♗b5 f5 4 ♘c3 ♘d4!?

An enterprising way to handle the opening and avoiding the main line linked to 4 ... fxe4 5 ♘xe4 d5.

5 ♗a4

a) 5 ♘xd4 exd4 6 ♘d5 c6 7 exf5 ♕g5 8 ♘c7+ ♔d8 9 ♘xa8 ♕xg2 10 ♖f1 cxb5 11 ♕e2 ♘f6 12 f4 ♕c6 13 ♔d1 d5 14 ♕d3 g6 15 ♕xd4 ♗xf5 16 ♕c3 ♗g4+ 17 ♔e1 ♗c5 0-1 Bauer-Held, Bundesliga 1990.

b) 5 exf5 ♘f6 6 ♘xe5 c6 7 ♗e2 ♕e7 8 ♘c4 d5 9 ♘e3 ♕f7 10 ♗d3 ♗d6 11 ♘e2 ♘xe2 12 ♗xe2 d4 13 ♘c4 ♗c7 14 d3 ♗xf5 15 ♗g5+= Hracek-Sokolov, Nussloch 1996.

c) 5 ♘xe5 ♕f6 6 f4 (6 ♘f3!?) 6 ... fxe4 7 d3 ♗b4 8 ♗a4 ♕h4+ 9 ♔f1 ♗xc3 10 bxc3 ♘e6 11 dxe4 ♘f6 12 ♘f3 ♕g4 13 h3 ♕g3=+ Schmitt-diel-Breutigam, Bundesliga 1997.

5 ... ♘f6 6 exf5 ♗c5 7 0-0 0-0 8 ♘xe5

It looks risky to grab another pawn at the expense of getting the rest of the pieces into play. In Foga-rasi-Aagaard, Budapest, White tried the calm 8 d3. White only had a slight edge after 8 ... d5 9 ♘xe5 ♗xf5 10 ♗f4 c6 11 ♗b3 a5 12 ♗g3 ♗d6 13 ♖e1 ♕c7 14 f4 ♔h8.

8 ... d5 9 ♘e2 ♕e7 10 ♘xd4 ♕xe5 11 ♘e2?

11 ♘b5 is essential.

11 ... ♘g4 12 g3 ♕xf5 13 ♘f4 g5 14 ♘d3

14 d4 gxf4 15 dxc5 ♘xh2! wins.

14 ... ♘xh2!

The knockout blow.

15 ♔xh2 ♕h3+ 16 ♔g1 ♕xg3+ 0-1

White resigned due to 17 ♔h1 ♕h4+ 18 ♔g1 ♖f6 19 ♗e8 ♗g4-+.

after 4 ... ♘d4

after 9 ♘e2

after 14 ♘d3

French: Exchange Variation 4 cxd5
Limbos-Bogart
Belgian Congo 1951

1 e4 e6 2 d4 d5 3 ♘c3 ♗b4 4 exd5

This is a version of the Exchange Variation, popular nowadays with Nogueiras and Short.

4 ... exd5 5 ♗d3

White's opening promises a small advantage with the possibility of building up a kingside attack. Probably a good choice when you are tackling a famous film star! Dr. Paul Limbos was playing friendly games against Humphrey Bogart during the filming of 'The African Queen'. Bogart was considered a decent club player but here he was waging a dollar a game against a Belgian international.

5 ... ♘f6

a) 5 ... c5 6 dxc5 ♘c6 7 a3 ♗xc5 8 ♘f3 ♘ge7 9 h3 0-0 10 0-0 h6 11 ♖e1+= Docx-Luminet, Antwerp 1997.

b) 5 ... ♘c6 6 a3 ♗xc3+ 7 bxc3 ♘ge7 8 ♕h5 ♗e6 9 ♖b1 b6 10 ♘f3 g6= De la Riva-Pecorelli Garcia, Havana 1998.

6 ♘ge2 0-0 7 0-0 c6 8 ♗g5 ♘bd7 9 ♘g3 ♕c7 10 ♘h5 ♘xh5 11 ♕xh5 g6 12 ♕h6 f5 13 ♖fe1 ♘b6 14 ♖e2 ♗d7?

This allows Limbos to speed up his attack. 14 ... ♕g7 15 ♖ae1 ♖f7 16 ♕h4 also maintains a strong initiative.

15 ♗e7!

White manages to transport a rook to the seventh rank.

15 ... ♗xe7 16 ♖xe7 ♖f7 17 ♖xf7 ♔xf7

The king goes for a walk.

18 ♕xh7+ ♔f6 19 ♖e1 ♕d6 20 g4 ♖d8 21 f4 g5 22 h4 1-0

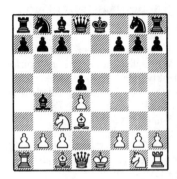

after 5 ♗d3

after 9 ♘g3

after 14 ... ♗d7

English: 3 e4
Mascarinas-Juarez Flores
Manila Interzonal 1990

1 c4 ♘f6 2 ♘c3 e6 3 e4

White has no desire to conform meekly with Black's plan of transposing to the Nimzo-Indian after 3 d4 ♗b4.

3 ... d5 4 e5 d4

Other moves:

a) 4 ... ♘e4 5 ♘xe4 dxe4 6 ♕g4 ♘c6 7 ♕xe4 ♕d4 8 ♕xd4 ♘xd4 9 ♗d3 ♗d7 10 ♘e2 ♗c5 11 b4 (11 ♗e4!?) 11 ... ♘xe2 12 ♔xe2 ♗d4 13 ♖b1 ♗xe5 ½-½ Bareev-Rozentalis, Kazan 1997.

b) 4 ... ♘fd7 5 d4 c5 6 cxd5 exd5 7 ♘f3 ♘c6 8 dxc5 ♗xc5 9 ♕xd5 ♕b6 10 ♗c4 ♗xf2+ 11 ♔e2 0-0 12 ♖f1 ♘dxe5 13 ♘xe5 ♘xe5 14 ♕xe5 ♗d4 15 ♕e4 ♗d7 16 ♘d5 ♕c5 17 ♔d3+- Azmaiparashvili-Mitkov, New York 1997.

5 exf6 dxc3 6 bxc3 ♕xf6 7 d4 c5 8 ♘f3 ♕d8?

This is not the best way to deal with 9 ♗g5. Instead Kasparov-Weemaes, Cannes simul 1988, continued with the usual 8 ... cxd4 but Black soon suffered after 9 cxd4 ♘c6 (9 ... ♗b4+!?) 10 a3 h6 11 ♗b2 ♗d6 12 ♗d3 0-0 13 0-0 e5 14 d5 ♘b8 15 c5! ♗xc5 16 ♘xe5 ♕f4 17 ♖c1 b6 18 ♖c4 ♕g5 19 h4 ♕d8 20 ♕f3 ♕d6 21 ♖f4 f5 22 ♘c4 ♕d7 23 ♖e1 ♗b7 24 ♗xf5 1-0

9 ♗d3! cxd4 10 cxd4 ♗b4+ 11 ♗d2 ♗xd2+ 12 ♕xd2 ♘d7 13 0-0 0-0 14 ♕f4 ♘f6 15 ♘e5 ♗d7 16 ♖fe1 ♖c8 17 ♖e3!

The rook can make a big impression by swinging across to g3 or h3 to aid a kingside attack.

17 ... ♗c6 18 ♖h3 h6 19 ♖e1 ♘e8 20 ♘g4 1-0

20 ... ♕g5 20 ♘xh6+ gxh6 22 ♖g3 wins.

after 3 e4

after 8 ♘f3

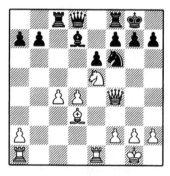

after 16 ... ♖c8

King's Indian Defence: Averbakh
Averbakh-Aronin
USSR Team Championship 1954

1 d4 ♘f6 2 c4 g6 3 ♘c3 ♗g7 4 e4 d6 5 ♗e2 0-0 6 ♗g5 c5 7 d5 h6 8 ♗f4

This model game by the originator of the system demonstrates White's attacking possibilities.

8 ... ♘bd7

Or:

a) 8 ... b5 9 cxb5 a6 10 a4 g5 11 ♗e3 ♕a5 12 ♗d2 ♕b4 13 f3 ♘h5 14 ♕c2 axb5 15 ♘d1 leaves the black queen trapped, Alburt-Wilder, USA Ch 1986.

b) 8 ... e6 9 dxe6 ♗xe6 10 ♗xd6 ♖e8 11 ♘f3 ♕b6 12 e5 ♘fd7 13 ♘b5 ♖c8 (13 ... ♘a6) 14 ♕b3 ♘c6 15 ♘c7 ♘cxe5 16 ♘xe5 ♘xe5 17 ♕xb6 axb6 18 ♘xa8± Alburt-Whitehead, New York 1987.

9 ♘f3 ♘g4 10 ♕d2 ♔h7 11 ♗g3 ♘ge5 12 ♘xe5 ♗xe5 13 f4 ♗d4 14 ♘b5 ♗f6 15 0-0 g5

The logic behind the text is fine because Black is battling for control of the e5 square. On the other hand one might rightly argue that the defensive pawn barrier is fatally weakened.

16 e5!

Averbakh grabs the chance to give away a pawn in order to exploit the b1-h7 diagonal.

16 ... dxe5

16 ... gxf4 leads to a speedy defeat upon 17 exf6 fxg3 18 ♗d3+ ♔g8 19 ♕xh6 ♘xf6 20 ♖xf6+-.

17 fxg5 ♗xg5 18 ♗d3+ ♔g7 19 ♕e2

A deadly threat is 20 ♕e4.

19 ... ♖h8 20 d6 e6 21 ♘c7 ♖b8 22 ♖xf7+ 1-0

Black resigned in view of 22 ... ♔xf7 23 ♕h5+ ♔g7 24 ♕g6+ ♔f8 25 ♘xe6 with mate to follow.

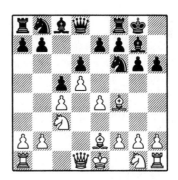

after 8 ♗f4

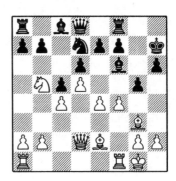

after 15 ... g5

after 21 ... ♖b8

Conclusion

A successful attack on the castled king requires good judgement, accurate calculation and perfect timing. Of course, an aggressive opening helps, such as that seen in Velicka-Souleidis where Black managed to introduce favourable complications and force White to concede critical weaknesses in his defensive pawn barrier.

Creating an open line for a rook along the h-file can be very effective against an opponent who has castled on the kingside. In the game, Polugaevsky-Kudrin, White manages to walk a tightrope by keeping his king in the centre while at the same time looking for a breakthrough on the kingside.

In situations of opposite-side castling, it is not an uncommon sight to see one careless move lead to ruin. In Mnatsakanian-Simagin, Black seizes his chance to conjure up a decisive counterattack out of nowhere.

The Art of Attack

1 Carry out a pawn storm to induce weaknesses in the opponent's defensive shield but bear in mind that any reckless advance can leave you vulnerable to a counterattack.

2 Speed up your attack by opening lines and diagonals.

3 Try to manoeuvre your pieces into an attacking formation in the minimum amount of moves. A space advantage is a big help if attacking forces have to be transferred from one side of the board to the other, since then there will be little or no distraction from counterplay.

The Art of Defence

1 One of the most difficult positions to break down is the castled king. Strengthen it still further with reinforcements available as a result of steady development.

2 Counter an attack on the flank by opening up the centre.

3 Watch out for sacrifices designed to destroy the king's pawn cover.

5 Checkmate in the Opening

It requires a certain amount of skill to deliver mate straight out of the opening! The defender will gladly give up material, anything to delay the inevitable, and this makes a swift victory even more sweet. Despite their spectacular nature, mating possibilities usually prompt a player to follow set procedures of play. Of course, other attacking methods are important too, but, when playing for mate, the astute player will take his cue from typically recurring mating patterns.

Colle-Buerger is an example of how a king can be caught by a standard sacrifice on h7—to crack the defence and follow up with an infiltration by the queen. By comparing it with, say, the game Aleksic-Solaja, White's sacrifice will be easier to find.

The more pieces on the board, the more the possibilities—and these extra possibilities can bring their own reward. This is evident in the game, Bronstein-Vedder, where White bamboozles his opponent with scintillating play, ending in a trademark mate.

Then again, it is a big mistake to go blindly on to the attack and sit back in expectation that the win will come all by itself. In Botos-Videki, White automatically pushes his pawns up the board only for the assault to falter. Black then takes advantage of White's resulting positional deficiencies to launch a counter-offensive.

Rogulj-Atlas features a frequently seen mating idea. The combination of the rook and bishop homing in on the king alerts Black to a decisive sacrifice.

Beliavsky-Larsen is a lesson in how to make the best use of pieces that are poised to strike deep into enemy territory. While Black is wasting time on an inappropriate flank pawn advance White's men get into position for a smashing breakthrough against the black king, stuck on its original square.

In Kobernat-Stenzel, White employs a tricky opening, sacrificing a pawn for rapid piece development and an initiative, and his early pursuit of the opposing king is crowned with success.

This chapter should encourage and convince you that certain techniques for checkmating early in the game can be learned.

Philidor: 5 ... ♗e7
Conquest-Wall
British Championship 1998

1 e4 e5 2 ♘f3 d6 3 d4 exd4

It is worth taking time-out to refute pages of analysis associated with 3 ... f5. After 4 ♘c3 the main line continues 4 ... fxe4 5 ♘xe4 d5 6 ♘eg5! h6 (6 ... e4 7 ♘e5 is bleak for Black) 7 ♘f7!! ♔xf7 8 ♘xe5+ with a devastating attack.

4 ♘xd4 ♘f6 5 ♘c3 ♗e7 6 ♗d3

White has investigated various ways to conduct the attack:

a) 6 ♗e2 0-0 7 0-0 c5 8 ♘b3 a6 9 f4 ♘c6 10 ♗e3 b5 11 ♗f3 ♕c7= Schmittdiel-Wall, Gent 1997.

b) 6 ♗c4 0-0 7 0-0 a6 8 a4 ♘c6 9 ♘xc6 bxc6 10 ♗f4 a5 11 ♕e2 ♘d7 12 e5 d5 13 ♗d3 ♘c5 gave Black a slight initiative in Mutton-Wall, British Championship 1998.

c) 6 ♗f4 0-0 7 ♕d2 ♘c6 8 0-0-0 ♘xd4 9 ♕xd4 ♗e6 10 f3 a6 11 ♕d2+= Lane-Wall, British Championship 1998.

6 ... 0-0 7 0-0 ♖e8 8 ♔h1 ♘c6 9 ♘xc6 bxc6 10 f4 ♗f8 11 e5 dxe5?!

11 ... ♘g4 is the only way to defend because now the open lines favour Conquest.

12 fxe5 ♘g4 13 ♗f4 ♕d7 14 ♕e1 ♕e6 15 ♕h4 h6?

15 ... ♘h6 is hardly appealing but was a sad necessity for Wall.

16 h3 g5 17 ♗xg5 hxg5 18 ♕h7 mate.

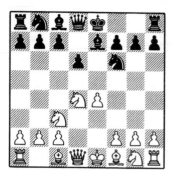

after 5 ... ♗e7

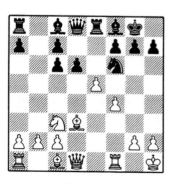

after 11 e5

after 15 ♕h4

Bogo-Indian: 6 ... c5
Bronstein-Vedder
Wijk aan Zee 1997

1 d4 ♘f6 2 c4 e6 3 ♘f3 b6 4 g3 ♗b7 5 ♗g2 ♗b4+

A tried and trusted way of avoiding the Queen's Indian Defence which is entered after 5 ... ♗e7.

6 ♗d2 c5

a) 6 ... ♗xd2+ 7 ♘bxd2 0-0 8 0-0 d6 9 ♕c2 c5 10 e4 cxd4 11 ♘xd4 ♘bd7 12 ♖ae1 a6 13 b3 ½-½ Farago-Eperjesi, Budapest 1997.

b) 6 ... ♕e7 7 ♘c3 c5 8 e3 0-0 9 0-0 d6 10 a3 ♗xc3 11 ♗xc3 ♘e4+= Vark-Rodrigues, Tallinn 1997.

7 dxc5 ♗xc5 8 0-0 0-0 9 ♘c3 ♘e4 10 ♕c2

A logical continuation which offers more practical chances than 10 ♘h4 ♘xc3 11 ♗xc3 ♗xg2 12 ♘xg2 ♘c6 when the game is equal.

10 ... f5 11 ♖ad1 ♘xd2 12 ♖xd2 a6 13 a3 ♕c7 14 ♖fd1 ♗e7 15 ♕b3 ♖c8 16 c5

A brilliant concept, jettisoning the c-pawn to increase the influence of the queen on the a2-g8 diagonal.

16 ... ♗c6

The tactics behind the sacrifice are revealed after 16 ... ♗xc5 when 17 ♖xd7! ♘xd7 18 ♕xe6+ ♔h8 19 ♕f7 ♖g8 20 ♖xb7+- is devastating.

17 cxb6 ♕b7 18 ♘e5! ♗xg2 19 ♖xd7 ♗d5

Or 19 ... ♘xd7 20 ♕xe6+ ♔h8 21 ♘f7+ ♔g8 22 ♘h6++ ♔h8 23 ♕g8+ ♖xg8 24 ♘f7 mate.

20 ♖1xd5 ♖xc3 21 ♖d8+

With typical grace, Bronstein conjures up a mating attack.

21 ... ♗f8 22 ♖xf8+ ♔xf8 23 ♕b4+ ♔e8 24 ♖d8+ ♔xd8 25 ♕f8 mate

after 5 ... ♗b4+

after 11 c5

after 20 ... ♖xc3

Spanish: 5 ... d6
Tal-Teschner
Vienna 1957

1 e4 e5 2 ♘f3 ♘c6 3 ♗b5 a6 4 ♗a4 ♘f6 5 0-0 d6 6 c3

6 ♗xc6+ bxc6 7 d4 is the Steinitz variation but the text offers more options for White.

6 ... ♗e7 7 d4 b5 8 ♗b3

This position can also arise after 1 e4 e5 2 ♘f3 ♘c6 3 ♗b5 a6 4 ♗a4 ♘f6 5 0-0 b5 6 ♗b3 ♗e7 7 d4 d6 8 c3—a move-order used to avoid the Marshall Gambit.

8 ... ♗g4

a) 8 ... 0-0 9 h3 ♘d7 10 ♗e3 ♘a5 11 ♗c2 ♘c4 12 ♗c1 c5 13 b3 ♘cb6 14 a4 led to a slight edge for White in Garcia-Van Riemsdijk, Buenos Aires 1997.

b) 8 ... exd4 9 cxd4 0-0 10 ♘c3 ♘a5 11 ♗c2 c5 12 h3 ♗b7 13 d5 ♖e8 14 ♘e2 ♗f8 15 ♘g3+= Joentausta-Sietioe, Lahti, 1996

9 h3 ♗xf3 10 ♕xf3 exd4 11 ♕g3

Teschner has captured a pawn but given his opponent a strong initiative—not the best pyschological choice considering that Tal was the greatest attacking player of his era!

11 ... g6

After 11 ... 0-0 12 ♗h6 with a clear advantage after 12 ... ♘h5 13 ♕g4 dxc3 14 ♘xc3 ♘d4 15 ♕xh5.

12 ♗d5 ♕d7 13 ♗h6 ♖b8

Black cannot castle kingside and 13 ... 0-0-0 14 a4! favours White.

14 f4 ♘d8 15 ♘d2 c6 16 ♗b3 dxc3 17 ♕xc3 ♕a7+ 18 ♔h1 ♕c5 19 ♕d3 ♘d7 20 e5 d5 21 f5 gxf5 22 ♕xf5 ♘f8 23 ♘e4! dxe4 24 ♖ac1 ♕b6 25 ♖cd1 1-0

Black resigned in view of 25 ... ♘fe6 26 ♗xe6 fxe6 27 ♕h5+ leads to mate.

after 5 ... d6

after 13 ♗h6

after 22 ... ♘f8

Kings Indian: 6 g4
Botos-Videki
Hungarian Team Champ. 1994

1 d4 ♘f6 2 c4 g6 3 ♘c3 ♗g7 4 e4 d6 5 ♗e2 0-0 6 g4!?
This bayonet attack, to kick-start the kingside offensive, is a big surprise weapon.

6 ... c5
Probably the best reply. Others:

a) 6 ... e5 7 d5 a5 8 h4 ♘e8 9 h5 f6 10 ♗e3 ♘a6 11 ♗d3 ♘c5 12 ♗c2 ♕e7 13 f3 ♖f7 14 ♘ge2 ♗f8 15 ♕d2 c6 16 0-0-0 gave White a strong attack in Quinteros-Ramis, Vicente Lopez 1993.

b) 6 ... c6 7 g5 ♘e8 8 h4 b5 9 cxb5 cxb5 10 ♗xb5 ♗b7 11 h5+= Siebrecht-Pehlgrim, Hamburg 1995.

7 d5 e6 8 g5 ♘e8 9 ♕d3
In Korchnoi-Cooper, Thessaloniki Olympiad 1988, White tried a positional approach with 9 ♘f3. The game continued 9 ... exd5 10 cxd5 ♘c7 11 ♕c2 b5 12 h4 ♗g4 13 ♘g1 ♗d7?! (13 ... ♗xe2 14 ♘gxe2 b4 looks a better bet for Black) 14 a4 bxa4 15 ♗f4 with a slight initiative.

9 ... exd5 10 cxd5 ♘c7 11 h4
A standard attacking pattern. If Black responds passively he will be swamped, but his hopes lie in the opponent's uncastled king disrupting the harmony of the white pieces.

11 ... ♖e8 12 ♗d2 b5 13 a3 ♕e7 14 f3 ♘ba6 15 ♘xb5 ♘xb5 16 ♕xb5 ♖b8 17 ♕a4 ♖xb2 18 ♗xa6 ♗xa6 19 ♖c1
Or 19 ♕xa6 ♖b6-+.

19 ... ♗b5 20 ♕a5 f5!
White's position is fatally flawed.

21 gxf6 ♗xf6 22 h5 ♗g5 23 ♖d1 0-1

after 6 g4

after 11 h4

after 20 ... f5

Fischer-Sozin Attack: 8 ♗g5
Yemelin-Nepomnishay
St.Petersburg Championship 1996

1 e4 c5 2 ♘f3 d6 3 d4 cxd4 4 ♘xd4 ♘f6 5 ♘c3 a6 6 ♗c4 e6 7 ♗b3 b5 8 ♗g5

The latest fashion is 8 f4 but the text is also tricky for Black.

8 ... ♗e7

a) 8 ... ♗e7 9 0-0 0-0 10 ♖e1 ♗b7 11 ♗xe6! fxe6 12 ♘xe6 ♕b6 13 ♘xf8 ♔xf8 14 ♗xf6 ♗xf6 15 ♘d5 ♗xd5 16 ♕xd5 ♕c6 17 ♕f5 h6 18 e5 dxe5 19 ♖ad1 led to a winning attack in Timmerman-De Vilder, Dieren 1997.

b) 8 ... ♘bd7 9 ♕e2 ♗b7 10 0-0-0 b4 11 ♘d5 ♘c5 12 e5 ♘xb3+ 13 ♘xb3 ♗xd5 14 ♖xd5 ♗e7 15 exf6 gxf6 16 ♗h4 exd5 17 ♗xf6 ♔d7 18 ♕g4+ ♔c7 19 ♗xh8 ♕xh8 20 ♕xb4+- Tate-De Firmian, Chicago 1995

9 ♕f3 ♕b6 10 0-0-0 0-0 11 ♗e3 ♕b7 12 g4 ♘c6 13 g5 ♘xd4 14 ♗xd4 ♘d7 15 ♕h5

Yemelin is happy to declare his aggressive intentions.

15 ... ♘c5

Any thoughts of winning the e-pawn with 15 ... b4? are spectacularly refuted by 16 ♘d5! exd5 (16 ... ♗d8 17 ♖hg1+-) 17 ♗xd5 ♕b8 18 g6! hxg6 19 ♕xg6 ♗f6 20 ♖hg1.

16 ♖hg1 ♖e8 17 ♖g3 ♘xb3+ 18 axb3 e5 19 ♘d5 g6 20 ♕h6 ♔h8 21 ♗xe5+!!

An incredible finish. White gives up a piece to open the d-file for the rook which plays a key role in the mating combination.

21 ... dxe5 22 ♘f6 1-0

Black had no wish to see 22 ... ♗xf6 23 gxf6 ♖g8 24 ♖d8! ♗e6 25 ♕g7 mate.

after 8 ♗g5

after 15 ♕h5

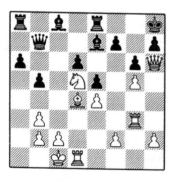

after 20 ... ♔h8

Colle: 4 ... ♗e7
Colle-Buerger
Hastings 1928

1 d4 ♘f6 2 ♘f3 e6 3 e3 d5 4 ♗d3

This system, perfected by the Belgian master Edgar Colle, is ideal for club players who want a reliable line without having to memorise lots of variations. Usually, the idea is to create a solid centre with c3, d4 and e3 and only later advance to e4.

4 ... ♗e7

a) 4 ... c5 5 c3 ♘c6 6 ♗d3 ♗d6 7 0-0 0-0 8 dxc5 ♗xc5 9 e4 e5? (9 ... ♕c7 10 ♕e2+=) 10 exd5 ♘xd5 11 ♘e4 ♗b6 12 ♗c4 ♗e6 13 ♘fg5 ♕d7 14 ♘xe6 fxe6 15 ♕g4 ♖ad8 16 ♗g5 ♘ce7 17 ♖ad1 ♖f5 18 ♗xe7+- Gehring-David, Baden-weiler 1995.

b) 4 ... ♗d6 5 ♘bd2 ♘bd7 6 0-0 c6?! (A natural but rather passive move. 6 ... c5 should be considered) 7 ♖e1 h6 8 ♕e2 0-0 9 e4 dxe4 10 ♘xe4 ♘xe4 11 ♕xe4 ♘f6 12 ♕h4 ♘d5 13 ♗g5 ♗e7 14 ♗xe7 ♕xe7 15 ♕g3 b6 16 ♘e5 ♗b7 17 ♖e4 ♖fd8 18 ♖h4 ♘f6 19 ♘g4 ♕e7 20 ♘xh6+ ♔f8 21 ♘f5 1-0 Siktanc-Korenek, Czech Team Ch. 1997.

5 ♘bd2 0-0 6 0-0 ♘bd7 7 e4 dxe4 8 ♘xe4 ♘xe4 9 ♗xe4 ♘f6 10 ♗d3 c5 11 dxc5 ♗xc5 12 ♗g5 ♗e7 13 ♕e2

Colle has the better development and a queenside pawn advantage.

13 ... ♕c7

Not 13 ... b6? which drops a piece after 14 ♗xf6 ♗xf6 15 ♕e4.

14 ♖ad1 ♖d8 15 ♘e5 ♗d7 16 ♗xh7+!

Superb.

16 ... ♔xh7 17 ♗xf6 ♗xf6 18 ♕h5+ ♔g8 19 ♕xf7+ 1-0

after 4 ♗d3

after 13 ♕e2

after 16 ♗xh7+

King's Gambit: 4 ... ♗g4
Rechel-Walendowski
Metz 1998

1 e4 e5 2 f4 exf4 3 ♘f3 d6 4 d4 ♗g4

4 ... g5 is more usual. Moroze-vich-Kasparov, Paris 1995, then continued 5 h4 g4 6 ♘g5 (6 ♘g1 is better) 6 ... h6 7 ♘xf7 ♔xf7 8 ♗xf4 ♗g7 9 ♗c4+ ♔e8 10 0-0 ♘c6 11 ♗e3 ♕xh4 12 ♖f7 ♖h7 13 e5 ♘a5 14 ♗d3 ♔xf7 15 ♕f1+ ♔e7 16 ♗xh7 ♗e6 when White's attack had fizzled out leaving him a piece down. The text, pinning the knight and preparing to castle queenside, is a natural way to proceed.

5 ♗xf4 ♘d7

Other ideas for Black include:

a) 5 ... ♘f6 6 ♘c3 ♗e7 7 ♗c4 0-0 8 0-0 c6 9 ♗b3 ♘bd7 10 ♕d3+= Aschauer-Sjoedahl, Vienna 1996.

b) 5 ... ♗e7 6 ♗d3 ♘c6 7 c3 ♘f6 8 0-0 ♘h5 9 ♗e3 0-0 10 ♘bd2 gave White the slightly better chances in Bohn-Ternette, Landau, 1988

6 ♗c4 ♕e7 7 0-0 0-0-0 8 ♘c3 ♘b6 9 ♗b3 h6 10 ♕d3 ♗e6 11 a4

Rechel strives to take advantage of his better development by quick-ly creating an attack on the queenside.

11 ... ♗xb3 12 cxb3 g5 13 ♗g3 ♗g7 14 a5 ♘d7 15 a6 b6 16 ♘d5 ♕e6 17 ♖fc1 c5 18 ♕b5!

White's constant probing has worked wonders because his oppo-nent's weakened defensive pawn barrier now collapses.

18 ... ♘b8 19 dxc5 dxc5 20 ♖xc5+ 1-0

after 4 ... ♗g4

after 11 a4

after 17 ... c5

French Winawer: 5 ... ♗a5
Rogulj-Atlas
Dresden Zonal 1998

1 e4 e6 2 ♘c3 d5 3 d4 ♗b4 4 e5 c5 5 a3 ♗a5

Rejecting the usual 5 ... ♗xc3+ for something more adventurous.

6 b4

a) 6 ♘f3 ♘c6 7 ♕d3 cxd4 8 ♘xd4 ♘ge7 9 b4 ♗b6 10 ♘xc6 bxc6 11 ♘a4 ♗c7 12 f4 a5 13 ♗e2 ♗a6 14 ♕d2 axb4 15 ♗xa6 ♖xa6 16 axb4 ♕a8-+ Voigt-Zehrfeld, Leipzig 1996.

b) 6 ♕g4 ♘e7 7 dxc5 ♗xc3+ 8 bxc3 ♕a5 9 ♗d2 ♘g6 10 h4 h5 11 ♕g5 ♘d7 12 c4 ♕a4= Lau-Vaganian, Bundesliga 1993.

c) 6 ♗d2 cxd4 7 ♘b5 ♗c7 8 f4 ♘c6 9 ♘f3 ♘h6 10 ♗d3 ♗d7 11 ♘fxd4 ♘xd4 12 ♘xd4 0-0 13 ♕h5 f5 14 h3 ♗b6 15 ♘e2 ♕e8 and Black has fended off the attack, Docx-Tondivar, Belgian Team Championship 1997.

6 ... cxd4 7 ♕g4 ♘e7 8 bxa5 dxc3 9 ♕xg7 ♖g8 10 ♕xh7 ♘bc6

Black's shattered kingside is compensated by his better development.

11 ♘f3 ♕c7 12 ♗b5 ♗d7 13 ♗xc6?!

It is better not to give Black a dominating bishop on the a8-h1 diagonal but play instead 13 0-0 as 13 ... ♘xe5 14 ♘xe5 ♕xe5 15 ♗xd7+ ♔xd7 16 ♕d3 leaves White sufficient compensation for the pawn due to the awkward position of the black king.

13 ... ♗xc6 14 0-0 d4 15 ♘g5 ♕xe5 16 ♕xf7+ ♔d7 17 ♕f4 ♖xg5 18 ♕xg5 ♖g8!!

A brilliant combination.

19 ♕xe5 ♖xg2+ 20 ♔h1 ♖xf2+ 21 ♔g1 ♖g2+ 22 ♔h1 ♖g3+ 0-1

after 5 a3

after 10 ... ♘bc6

after 18 ♕xg5

Old Indian: 5 ♗g5
Tsesarsky-Khasin
Kfar Saba 1997

1 ♘f3 d6 2 d4 ♘d7 3 c4 ♘gf6 4 ♘c3 e5 5 ♗g5!?

The standard move is 5 e4 but the text has the potential to create problems for Black at a very early stage.

5 ... ♗e7

Others:

a) 5 ... h6 6 ♗h4 ♗e7 7 e3 0-0 8 ♕c2 exd4 9 ♘xd4 ♖e8 10 0-0-0 ♗f8 11 g4 c6 12 ♘f5 ♕c7 13 g5 hxg5 14 ♗xg5 ♘h7 15 ♖g1+= Ginsburg-Brooks, Philadelphia 1989.

b) 5 ... c6 6 e3 ♕a5 (threatening 7 ... e4) 7 ♗h4 ♗e7 8 ♕c2 0-0 9 ♗d3 ♖e8 10 0-0 ♘f8 11 dxe5 dxe5 12 ♗g3 ♗d8 13 h3 ♗c7 14 a3 ♕c5 15 b4 left White a space advantage in Delemarre-Cifuentes,Wijk aan Zee 1995.

6 ♕c2 c6 7 0-0-0 ♕c7 8 e3 0-0 9 ♗d3 h6 10 h4 ♖e8 11 g4 ♘f8?

Now is the time to snatch the bishop with 11 ... hxg5 when White will proceed 12 hxg5 e4 13 ♘xe4 ♘xg4 14 ♘g3 ♘f8 15 ♗h7+ ♔h8 16 ♗f5+ ♔g8 17 ♖h4 ♘h6 18 gxh6 ♗xh4 19 ♘xh4 g6 20 ♗e4 with a slight advantage. 11 ... exd4!? is also possible.

12 ♗xf6 ♗xf6 13 g5 ♗g4 14 gxf6! ♗xf3 15 ♖dg1!

The best and most aggressive option.

15 ... ♗xh1

15 ... g6 does nothing to stop the stampede towards the king after 16 ♗xg6! fxg6 (16 ... ♔h8 17 ♖h3+-) 17 ♖xg6+ ♘xg6 18 ♕xg6+ ♔h8 19 f7 winning.

16 ♗h7+ ♘xh7 17 ♖xg7+ 1-0

after 5 ♗g5

after 9 ♗d3

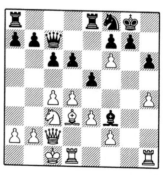

after 14 ... ♗xf3

Caro-Kann: Main Line
Beliavsky-Larsen
Tilburg 1981

1 e4 c6 2 d4 d5 3 ♘c3 dxe4 4 ♘xe4 ♗f5 5 ♘g3 ♗g6 6 h4 h6 7 ♘f3 ♘d7 8 h5 ♗h7 9 ♗d3 ♗xd3

In the game Beliavsky-Larsen, London 1984, Black tried 9 ... ♘gf6?! which merely disrupted his kingside development. The game continued: 10 ♗xh7 ♘xh7 11 ♕e2 e6 12 ♗d2 ♗e7 13 0-0-0 ♕b6 14 ♘e5 ♖d8 15 ♖he1 0-0 16 ♘g6! (this attacking theme is borrowed from the main illustrative game) 16 ... ♖fe8 17 ♘xe7+ ♖xe7 18 ♘f5 ♖ee8 19 ♘d6 ♖f8 20 ♗f4 ♘df6 21 ♗e5±.

10 ♕xd3 ♘gf6 11 ♗f4 e6 12 0-0-0 ♗e7 13 ♘e5 a5?! 14 ♖he1 a4?

A typical pawn lunge which is refuted by means of a stunning combination.

15 ♘g6! ♘d5

If 15 ... fxg6 White has a strong attack according to Beliavsky after 16 ♕xg6+ ♔f8 17 ♖xe6 ♕e8 18 ♖de1 ♕xg6 19 hxg6 ♗b4 20 ♘f5.

16 ♘f5 ♗f8 17 ♗d6 ♖g8

17 ... fxg6 fails to 18 ♘xg7+! ♔xf7 19 ♕xg6+ ♔g8 20 ♘e6+ ♗g7 21 ♕xg7 mate.

18 c4 ♘b4 19 ♕h3!

The threat of 20 ♘xh6! gxh6 21 ♖xe6+ is decisive.

19 ... fxg6 20 ♖xe6+ ♔f7 21 hxg6+ ♔xe6 22 ♖e1+ ♘e5 23 ♗xe5 1-0

after 9 ♗d3

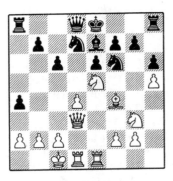

after 14 ... a4

after 18 ... ♘b4

Owen's Defence: 4 f4
Aleksic-Solaja
Croatian Team Championship 1998

1 e4 b6 2 d4 e6 3 ♗d3 ♗b7 4 f4!?

Black no doubt expected 4 ♘f3 but this old idea has tremendous surprise value.

4 ... ♘f6

A look at history reveals that in the game Pillsbury-Hodges, Cambridge Springs 1904, Black tried 4 ... ♗e7 before putting pressure on the centre. The game continued: 5 ♘f3 c5 6 ♗e3 (6 c3!?) 6 ... .c4 7 ♗xc4 ♗xe4 8 ♘c3 ♗b4 9 0-0 ♗xc3 10 bxc3 ♕c7 11 ♘d2 ♘f6 12 ♘xe4 ♘xe4 13 ♕d3 d5 14 ♗b5+ ♘d7 15 c4 when White's intiative gave him a small advantage.

5 ♕e2 c5 6 c3 ♗e7

Wagner-Wenzel, Bundesliga 1988, saw instead 6 ... cxd4 7 cxd4 d5 8 e5 ♘e4 9 ♘f3 ♗b4+ 10 ♗d2 ♘xd2 11 ♘bxd2 ♗xd2+ 12 ♘xd2 0-0 13 0-0 ♘c6 14 ♘f3 g6 15 a3 ♖c8 16 ♕f2 when Black had weak dark squares around his king which led rapidly to his downfall.

7 ♘f3 d5 8 e5 ♘e4 9 0-0 0-0 10 ♘bd2

White prepares to exchange Black's central knight which will strengthen the light-squared bishop and enable him to use his space advantage to start an attack.

10 ... ♘xd2 11 ♗xd2 ♕d7 12 ♘g5 ♗xg5 13 fxg5 ♘c6 14 ♖f4 ♘e7 15 ♗xh7+!

Exposing the king in text book fashion.

15 ... ♔xh7 16 ♕h5+ ♔g8 17 ♖h4 f6 18 gxf6 ♖fc8 19 ♕h7+ 1-0

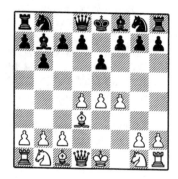

after 4 f4

after 10 ♘bd2

after 14 ... ♘e7

Dutch: Ilyin-Zhenevsky 7 ♕c2
Cherepkov-Grishanovich
St Petersburg Championship 1997

**1 d4 e6 2 c4 f5 3 ♘f3 ♘f6 4 g3
♗e7 5 ♗g2 d6 6 ♘c3 0-0 7 ♕c2**

A little move-order trick which delays castling in order firstly to open up the centre.

7 ... ♕e8?!

This is the normal plan intending ... ♗d8 and ... e5, but the change in circumstances requires a different approach. For instance, Kindl-Gorgs, Stuttgart 1985, saw Black play 7 ... ♘c6 to exploit the position of the queen: 8 d5 ♘b4 9 ♕b3 ♘a6 10 dxe6 ♘c5 11 ♕c2 ♗xe6 12 ♘d4 ♗xc4 13 ♘a4 (13 ♘xf5=) 13 ... ♗d5 14 ♗xd5+ ♘xd5 15 ♘xc5 dxc5 16 ♘e6 ♘e3 17 ♗xe3 ♕d5 18 0-0 ♕xe6 19 ♗xc5 ♖f7 ½-½.

**8 e4 ♕h5 9 e5 ♘e8 10 ♘e2 ♘c6
11 ♘f4 ♕f7 12 h4**

With this advance of the h-pawn, White declares his kingside attacking intentions.

12 ... ♖b8 13 a3 ♔h8

13 ... ♘xd4, as a simplifying device, is flawed upon 14 ♘xd4 dxe5 15 ♘dxe6 ♗xe6 16 ♘xe6 ♕xe6 17 ♗d5 winning.

**14 ♗e3 g6?! 15 0-0-0 ♗d7 16 h5
♔g8**

Black has the miserable choice of 16 ... g5 17 ♘g6+! winning the exchange or 16 ... gxh5 17 ♖xh5 when White can double the rooks on the h-file with a winning game.

**17 hxg6 hxg6 18 ♖h6 ♔g7 19
♖dh1 b5 20 ♖h7+ ♔g8 21 ♖h8+
♔g7 22 ♖1h7 mate.**

after 7 ♕c2

after 12 h4

after 16 h5

Advance French: 6 ♗d3
Kobernat-Stenzel
Hawaii 1998

**1 e4 e6 2 d4 d5 3 e5 c5 4 c3 ♘c6
5 ♘f3 ♕b6 6 ♗d3**

The idea of sacrificing at least the d-pawn was popularised by Sir Stuart Milner-Barry. It is appealing to those who relish swashbuckling attacks and feared by Black if he is unfamiliar with the ensuing complications.

6 ... cxd4 7 cxd4 ♗d7

Some players still fall for 7 ... ♘xd4?? 8 ♘xd4 ♕xd4 9 ♗b5+ winning the queen.

8 ♘c3 ♘xd4 9 ♘xd4 ♕xd4 10 0-0 ♕xe5

In Ayas-Hernandez, Vendrell 1996, Black preferred the cautious 10 ... a6 when White was on top after 11 ♕e2 ♘e7 12 ♔h1 ♘c6 13 f4 ♘b4 14 ♖d1 ♘xd3 15 ♖xd3 ♕c4 16 b3 ♕c7 17 ♗b2 b5 18 f5! (the strength of this move was first revealed in a joint analysis with Jon Ady in my book *Beating the French*) 18 ... ♗e7 19 f6 ♗d8 20 fxg7 ♖g8 21 ♖g3 ♕b7 22 ♕h5 ♗b6 23 ♖c1 ♗c6 24 ♕xh7+-.

11 ♖e1 ♕d6 12 ♘b5 ♗xb5

If 12 ... ♕b6 then 13 ♗e3 ♕a5 14 ♗d2 ♕d8 15 ♖c1 ♖c8 16 ♖xc8 ♕xc8 17 ♕b3 ♘f6 18 ♖c1 ♗c6 19 ♘xa7 ♕d8 20 ♘xc6 bxc6 21 ♖xc6 left White with a powerful pair of passed pawns, Antonsson-Johansson, Vaxjo 1992.

13 ♗xb5+ ♔d8 14 ♕h5! g6 15 ♕f3 f5 16 ♗f4 ♕e7 17 ♖ac1 ♗g7 18 ♗c7+ ♕xc7 19 ♕xd5+ ♔c8 20 ♕d7+ 1-0

after 6 ♗d3

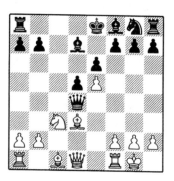

after 10 0-0

after 17 ... ♗g7

King's Fianchetto: 3 b4
Larsen-Olafsson
Beverwijk 1959

1 g3 e5 2 ♗g2 d5 3 b4?!
Bent Larsen has always had an independent spirit and here he comes up with something different as early as move 3! Instead of the usual 3 c4 he tries to enter a sort of Sokolsky and rely on the power of his fianchettoed bishops to undermine the central pawns.

3 ... ♗xb4
A look through the archives indicates that few players have enough courage to accept the gambit. However, Slipak-Sorokin, San Fernando 1993, saw a very strong Russian player surprisingly decline the offered pawn with 3 ... ♘f6. The game continued: 4 ♗b2 ♗d6 5 c4 c6 6 ♕b3 dxc4 7 ♕xc4 ♗e6 8 ♕c2 ♘bd7 9 ♘f3 0-0 10 0-0 ♕e7 11 d3 ♘d5 12 a3 a5 13 bxa5 ♖xa5 14 ♘bd2 ♘5b6 15 ♗c3 ♖xa3 16 ♖xa3 ♗xa3 17 ♘xe5 ♘xe5 18 ♗xe5 with equal chances.

4 c4 ♗e6
Not 4 ... dxc4?? when 5 ♕a4+ ♘c6 6 ♗xc6+ wins.

5 ♗b2 ♘c6 6 f4 ♘ge7 7 ♘f3 d4
Olafsson returns the pawn in order to go on the attack.

8 ♘xe5 ♘xe5 9 fxe5 0-0 10 ♕c2 ♘g6 11 ♗xb7 ♖b8 12 ♗e4 f5!
An energetic continuation which forces White on the defensive or dares him to open up the f-file.

13 ♗d3 ♘xe5 14 0-0 ♗c5 15 ♗a3 ♕d6 16 ♗xc5 ♕xc5 17 ♕c1 f4 18 gxf4 ♘xd3 19 exd3 ♗h3 20 ♖f3 ♕h5 21 ♖g3 ♖xf4
Olafsson intends to triple on the f-file and White is a mere spectator.

22 ♘a3 ♖bf8 23 ♘c2 ♕f5 0-1

after 3 b4

after 12 ... f5

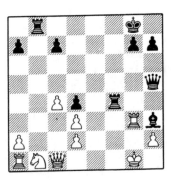

after 21 ... ♖xf4

Semi-Slav: 9 ♗e2
Sakaev-Kobalija
Russian Championship 1998

1 d4 d5 2 ♘f3 ♘f6 3 c4 c6 4 ♘c3 e6 5 ♗g5 h6 6 ♗h4 dxc4 7 e4 g5 8 ♗g3 b5 9 ♗e2

A move that has been left in the shadows by the alternatives 9 a3, 9 h4 and 9 ♕c2.

9 ... b4?!

a) 9 ... ♗b4 10 ♕c2 ♗b7 11 0-0 ♘bd7 12 ♘e5 h5 13 h3 h4 14 ♗h2 ♘h5 15 ♗xh5 ♖xh5 16 ♖ad1 ♕e7 17 ♘xd7 ♕xd7 18 d5 cxd5 19 exd5 ♗xc3 20 ♕xc3 ♗xd5 21 ♖fe1 ½-½ Lalic-Zhu Chen, Ubeda 1998.

b) 9 ... a6 10 ♕c2 ♗e7 11 ♖d1 ♗b7 12 0-0 ♘bd7 13 ♘e5 ♘xe5 14 ♗xe5 ♖g8 15 ♗xf6 ♗xf6 16 e5 ♗e7 17 ♕h7± Lobron-Slobodjan, Nussloch 1996.

10 ♘a4 ♘xe4 11 ♗e5 ♘f6 12 ♘c5

White has had mixed results after 12 ♗xc4 but the text is likely to put 9 ... b4 out of business. The idea is to prevent Black from getting rid of the bishop on e5 with a later ... ♘bd7 because now the knight on d7 can simply be exchanged.

12 ... ♗g7

After 12 ... ♗xc5 13 dxc5 ♘bd7 14 ♗d6 White is better because the black king is stuck in the centre.

13 ♗xc4 0-0 14 ♕c2 ♘bd7 15 h4 gxh4 16 ♘xd7! ♗xd7 17 ♖xh4 ♘d5 18 ♗xg7 ♔xg7 19 ♖g4+ ♔h8 20 ♕d2

The attack is devastatingly simple.

20 ... ♕f6 21 ♘e5 ♗e8 22 0-0-0 ♘e7 23 ♖h1 ♘g8 24 ♖gh4 ♔g7 25 ♖f4 1-0

Black resigned due to 25 ... ♕e7 26 ♖g4+ ♔h7 27 ♖xg8 ♔xg8 28 ♕xh6 with mate to follow.

after 9 ♗e2

after 12 ♘c5

after 19 ... ♔h8

Conclusion

A successful offensive, culminating in checkmate right out of the opening, requires not only a knowledge of standard mating patterns, but also the ability to co-ordinate one's forces in such a way that they can carry out a lightning attack.

Though a surprise opening can reap rich rewards, any neglect of basic chess principles, such as development of pieces, can be suicidal. Larsen-Olafsson is a good example of how badly things can go wrong when imagination runs wild.

An illustration of how checkmate can be the well-deserved prize for the successful execution of a logical plan is seen in Rechel-Walendowski. Here White consistently strives to undermine Black's defensive shell and is finally rewarded with a decisive weakening of the light squares, allowing his queen to invade and conquer.

The Art of Attack

1 Remember, an aggressive opening is a big help if you want to go for an early checkmate.

2 If possible, demolish the enemy king's defensive wall by a piece sacrifice—this is often the best way to corner the king.

3 Learn typical mating patterns. This will help you spot the moment to go on the offensive.

The Art of Defence

1 Be prepared to accept sacrifices gratefully and win with the extra material. Many players want to attack all the time and are too free with their material.

2 Castle and get the king out of the centre.

3 Avoid passive positions. Always look at ways of creating counterplay to sidetrack attackers from their main objective—your king!

6 Winning Moves

An effective way to sharpen your tactical skill is to study games with different kinds of combinations, which will alert you to all sorts of opportunities for winning moves.

It is all very well solving a 'White to play and mate in two' newspaper puzzle in the comfort of your own home but it is a quite different proposition when you are thrown on your own resources in over-the-board play. That is why examples such as Van der Wiel-Saunders and Uhlmann-Dunnington are so useful, since they illustrate how tactics can flow naturally from a positional advantage. Knowing how to formulate a plan will enable an attacker to steer a game towards a position where, at a given moment, there is a possibility of playing a winning combination.

Some decisive moves dazzle with their elegance as is the case with the exceptional queen sacrifice seen in Liu Wen Che-Donner. However, one should not forget the importance of the preceding moves, which entail active piece play and probing of the defence, as without these the final attack would not have been possible. Also the fact that winning moves stem from recurring combinational themes will encourage you to learn and apply these attacking techniques in your own games.

Sometimes a decisive blow is delivered just at the moment when the opponent appears to have set up a rock-solid defence, as in Karpov-Hort and Emms-Sjodahl. Nevertheless, it is not mere chance that White is still able to sacrifice because, if we look closely, we see that he has advantages such as a superiority in space and better development.

In the games Kudrin-Fedorowicz, Crickmore-P.Lane and Carlier-Kerhoff the critical moment arrives at a very early stage, showing how pressure in the opening can pay handsome dividends. The King's Gambit has a deserved reputation as an attacking weapon and this is amply illustrated in Grabarczyk-Shetty. White uses his lead in development to line up an impressive array of pieces against the black king and a decisive breakthrough is not long in coming. The merits of employing a tricky opening are borne out by Svensen-Reefschlaeger where Black employs the rather unusual Chigorin Defence and has the better game after just five moves!

If you think that you have to enter a complicated melée to create the necessary conditions for a successful attack—then don't panic! The games Kuprechik-Romanishin and Bolzoni-Lane demonstrate that even in tranquil positions there are latent possibilities just waiting to be unleashed.

Hopefully, by studying the various themes depicted here, you will be able to reach winning positions and play winning moves in your own games.

Petroff: 3 d4
Van der Wiel-Saunders
Breda 1998

1 e4 e5 2 ♘f3 ♘f6 3 d4 ♘xe4 4 ♗d3 d5 5 ♘xe5 ♘d7 6 ♘xd7 ♗xd7 7 0-0 ♗e7

An easy and popular alternative to the well-known lines starting with 7 ... ♕h4.

8 c4

The best way to proceed is to undermine the d5 pawn in order to weaken the knight on e4.

8 ... c6

Logically supporting the pawn.

J.Polgar-Van der Sterren, Wijk aan Zee 1998, saw Black retreat the knight after which he could do nothing to stop White's pieces breaking through on the queenside. That game continued 8 ... ♘f6 9 ♘c3 ♗e6 10 c5 0-0 11 ♗f4 c6 12 b4 ♕d7 13 ♕c2 g6 14 b5 ♖fe8 15 a4 ♘h5 16 ♗e3 ♗d8 17 a5+=.

9 ♘c3 ♘xc3 10 bxc3 dxc4 11 ♗xc4 0-0 12 ♖e1 ♗f5 13 ♕f3 ♗g6 14 ♗f4 ♗d6 15 ♗xd6 ♕xd6 16 h4

A sure sign of a class player. Van der Wiel makes maximum use of his space advantage by taking time out to push the h-pawn and drive the enemy bishop away from the defence of f7.

16 ... h6 17 ♖e5 ♕d7 18 h5 ♗h7 19 ♖ae1

White has a huge positional advantage. The rook threatens to invade on the seventh rank and this cannot be prevented without loss of material.

19 ... ♖fe8 20 ♕xf7+! 1-0

after 7 ... ♗e7

after 13 ♕f3

after 19 ... ♖fe8

Caro-Kann: 4 ... ♘d7
Karpov-Hort
Bugojno 1978

1 e4 c6 2 d4 d5 3 ♘d2 dxe4 4 ♘xe4 ♘d7 5 ♘f3 ♘gf6 6 ♘xf6+ ♘xf6 7 ♘e5 ♗f5!?

An interesting alternative to 7 ... ♗e6 or 7 ... ♘d7.

8 c3 e6

If 8 ... ♘d7 then 9 ♘xf7 ♔xf7 10 ♕f3 e6 11 g4 ♕f6 12 gxf5 ♕xf5 13 ♕e3 left Black's king vulnerable in Kavalek-Barcza, Caracas 1971.

9 g4 ♗g6

In the game Thipsay-Sandipan, Calcutta 1998, Black encouraged White to chase the bishop: 9 ... ♗e4 10 f3 ♗g6 11 h4 h6 (the point is that 11 ... h5 is less effective now that the pawn on f3 supports g4) 12 ♘xg6 fxg6 13 ♗d3 ♗d6 14 ♗xg6+ ♔d7 15 ♕b3+-.

10 h4 h5

If 10 ... ♗d6 then 11 ♕e2! ♗xe5? (11 ... c5!?) 12 dxe5 ♕d5 13 ♖h3 ♘xg4 14 ♕xg4 ♕xe5+ 15 ♖e3+- Mecking-Miles, Wijk aan Zee 1978.

11 g5 ♘d5 12 ♘xg6 fxg6 13 ♕c2 ♔f7 14 ♖h3 ♘e7 15 ♗c4 ♘f5 16 ♖f3 ♕d7 17 ♖xf5+!

A brilliant sacrifice which annihilates Black's defence.

17 ... gxf5 18 ♕xf5+ ♔e7 19 ♕e4 ♖e8 20 ♗f4 ♔d8 21 ♕e5 ♖g8 22 0-0-0 g6 23 ♖e1 ♗g7 24 ♕b8+ ♔e7

A better try is 24 ... ♕c8 but 25 ♕xa7 ♖e7 26 ♕a5+ ♔d7 27 ♕c5 also looks terrible for Black.

25 ♖xe6+! 1-0

Black had no wish to see 25 ... ♕xe6 26 ♕c7+ ♕d7 27 ♗d6 mate.

after 4 ... ♗f5

after 10 h4

after 16 ... ♕d7

King's Indian: Four Pawns 9 e5
Crickmore-P.Lane
Paignton 1996

1 d4 ♘f6 2 c4 g6 3 ♘c3 ♗g7 4 e4 d6 5 f4 0-0 6 ♘f3 c5 7 d5 e6 8 ♗e2 exd5 9 e5!?

Recent books on the King's Indian assume 9 cxd5 is the only move. But after the tricky text Black must defend very accurately.

9 ... ♘e4

It is easy to go wrong:

a) 9 ... ♘g4 10 cxd5 dxe5 11 h3 e4 12 hxg4 exf3 13 gxf3 ♖e8 14 f5 ♘d7 15 ♗h6 ♗xh6 16 ♖xh6 ♕g5 17 ♕d2 ♕xd2+ 18 ♔xd2 gxf5 19 gxf5 ♔g7 20 ♖d6 ♘b6 21 ♖g1+ ♔f8 22 ♖g5 ♗d7 23 ♖h6+- Kouatly-Jadoul, Montpellier 1985.

b) 9 ... dxe5 10 fxe5 ♘e8 11 cxd5 ♗f5 12 0-0 a6 13 ♗g5 f6 14 ♗h4 g5 15 ♗g3 fxe5 16 ♘xe5 ♘d6 17 ♗g4 b5 18 ♗xf5 ♘xf5 19 ♕g4± Marinin-Kazakov, St Petersburg 1998.

10 cxd5 ♘xc3 11 bxc3 ♘d7

At this point Lane (no relation) had spent a lot of time on the opening. There was no need to consult a computer because on the notice board there was last year's best game, Crickmore-Cole, Four Pawns Attack, 25 moves 1-0.

12 e6 ♗xc3+ 13 ♗d2 ♗xa1 14 ♕xa1

White now dominates the important a1-h8 diagonal.

14 ... fxe6 15 dxe6 ♘b6 16 ♘g5 ♕f6 17 ♗c3 ♕e7 18 ♗h8 h6 19 h4! ♖xf4

After 19 ... hxg5 20 hxg5 White moves his bishop and plays ♖h8+.

20 g3 ♖f8 21 h5 d5 22 hxg6 d4 23 ♘f7 ♖xf7 24 gxf7+ ♔xh8 25 ♕c1 1-0

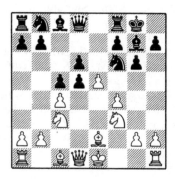

after 9 e5

after 14 ♕xa1

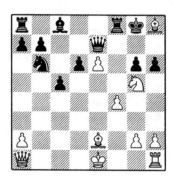

after 18 ... h6

French Tarrasch: 3 ... c5
Emms-Sjodahl
Harplinge 1998

**1 e4 e6 2 d4 d5 3 ♘d2 c5 4 ♘gf3
cxd4 5 exd5 ♕xd5 6 ♗c4 ♕d6 7
0-0 a6?!**

7 ... ♘f6 is standard after which
Emms would presumably have
transposed into the main line after 8
♘b3 ♘c6 9 ♘bxd4 ♘xd4 10 ♘xd4
♘f6. Another move-order, 7 ...
♘c6, is a mistake because of 8 ♘e4
followed by recapturing on d4. e.g.
8 ... ♕d8 9 ♕e2 ♗e7 10 ♖d1 ♘f6
11 c3 ♘xe4 12 ♕xe4 0-0 13 cxd4
♘b4 14 ♖e1 ♗f6 15 ♗f4 ♘d5 16
♗e5 ♗xe5 17 dxe5 b6 18 ♗xd5
♕xd5 19 ♕xd5 exd5 20 ♖ac1 ♗e6
21 ♘d4±. Del Campo-Escobedo
Tinajero, Mexico City 1991. 7 ...
♘e7 is also unconvincing. Pizzato
-Zakarias, Szeged 1994, continued
8 ♘e4 ♕c7 9 ♘xd4 ♘f5 10 ♗g5
♘xd4 (10 ... ♕xc4 11 ♘xf5+-) 11
♕xd4 ♘c6 12 ♗b5 ♗d7 13 ♕c3
♖c8 14 ♖ad1 ♘e5? 15 ♕xe5! 1-0

**8 ♘e4 ♕c7 9 ♕xd4 ♘c6 10 ♕c3
♗d7 11 ♖d1**

The opening has been a complete
success for White. He has greater
space and can develop fluently. A
bonus is that Black does not have
time to whisk his king to safety on
the kingside.

**11 ... b5 12 ♗b3 b4 13 ♕c4 ♘f6
14 ♘xf6+ gxf6 15 ♗f4 ♕b6 16
♖xd7!**

The breakthrough.

16 ... ♔xd7 17 ♖d1+ ♔c8

17 ... ♔e7 18 ♖d6 ♖c8 19 ♖xe6+
fxe6 20 ♕xe6+ ♔d8 21 ♕xf6+
wins.

**18 ♘d4 ♔b7 19 ♘xe6 ♖e8 20
♖d7+ ♔c8 21 ♖xf7 ♖e7 22 ♖xe7
♗xe7 23 ♗a4 ♔b7 24 ♗e3 1-0**

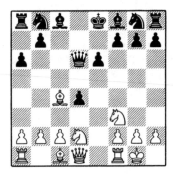

after 7 ... a6

after 11 ♖d1

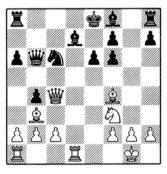

after 15 ... ♕b6

Pirc: Chinese Attack 5 g4
Liu Wen Che-Donner
Buenos Aires Olympiad 1978

1 e4 d6 2 d4 ♘f6 3 ♘c3 g6 4 ♗e2 ♗g7 5 g4

After this famous game the line became known as the Chinese attack. Other options are:

a) 5 ... c6 6 g5 ♘fd7 7 f4 h6 8 ♘f3 b5 9 ♗e3 b4 10 ♘a4 ♘b6 11 gxh6 ♗xh6 12 ♘xb6 ♕xb6 13 ♕d2= Vasiukov-Miller, Bad Liebenzell 1996.

b) 5 ... ♘c6 6 g5 ♘d7 7 ♗e3 e5 8 ♘f3 exd4 9 ♘xd4 0-0 10 h4 ♘xd4 11 ♗xd4 ♗xd4 12 ♕xd4 ♘b6 13 0-0-0 ♗e6 14 f4 f5 15 h5 gave White strong attacking chances on the h-file in Schulz-Woelbert, Dortmund 1991.

c) 5 ... c5 6 g5 ♘fd7 7 d5 ♘a6 8 f4 ♖b8 9 ♘f3 b5 10 h4 ♘c7 11 h5 b4 12 h6 ♗f8 13 ♘b1 ♘b6 14 b3+= Todor-Holzer, Austrian Team Championship 1996.

5 ... h6?! 6 h3 c5 7 d5 0-0?!

Black probably took 6 h3 as a sign that White had no intention of going on the offensive.

8 h4 e6 9 g5 hxg5 10 hxg5 ♘e8?!

10 ... ♘h7 should be considered.

11 ♕d3

The queen prepares to transfer to the h-file with deadly effect.

11 ... exd5 12 ♘xd5 ♘c6 13 ♕g3 ♗e6 14 ♕h4 f5 15 ♕h7+ ♔f7 16 ♕xg6+

Brilliant. With this impressive sacrifice, the black king is led to the slaughter.

16 ... ♔xg6 17 ♗h5+ ♔h7 18 ♗f7+ ♔h6 19 g6+ ♔g7

If 19 ... ♔h8 then 20 ♖xh6+ ♔g7 21 ♖h7 mate.

20 ♗xh6+ 1-0

after 5 g4

after 11 ♕d3

after 15 ... ♔f7

King's Gambit:
Fischer Defence 4 ♗c4
Grabarczyk-Shetty
Koszalin 1998

1 e4 e5 2 f4 exf4 3 ♘f3 d6 4 ♗c4 h6 5 h4

A slightly different approach to the alternatives 5 d4 and 5 d3. It is designed to prevent ... g7-g5.

5 ... ♘f6

Other approaches are:

a) 5 ... ♗e6 6 ♗xe6 fxe6 7 d4 ♕f6 8 e5 ♕f5 9 ♕d2 ♘c6 10 ♕xf4 ♕xc2 11 0-0 0-0-0 12 ♕f7 ♕f5 13 ♘g5 Rechel-Michalczak, Bundesliga 1994.

b) 5 ... ♗g4 6 d4 ♘c6 7 ♗xf4 ♘f6 8 ♘c3 ♗e7 9 ♕d2 a6 10 a3 ♗xf3 11 gxf3 ♘d7 12 0-0-0 ♗f6 13 ♗e3+= Langheinrich-Toivanen, Vaxjo 1992.

6 ♘c3 ♗g4 7 d4 ♗e7 8 ♗xf4 ♘h5 9 ♗e3 ♘g3 10 ♖h2 c6 11 ♕d3

White has managed to take a lead in development without being the customary pawn down.

11 ... b5 12 ♗b3 a5 13 a4 b4 14 ♘d1 0-0 15 ♗f2 ♘h5 16 ♘e3 ♘f4 17 ♕d2 ♘xg2+ 18 ♖xg2 ♗xf3 19 ♖xg7+!

A brilliant combination which exposes Black's disorganisation.

19 ... ♔h8

If 19 ... ♔xg7 White triumphs in style after 20 ♘f5+ ♔g8 21 ♕xh6 ♗f6 22 ♔d2! and Black will be mated.

20 ♘f5 ♗g5 21 hxg5 ♗g4 22 g6 ♕g5 23 ♕xg5 hxg5 24 ♖h7+ ♔g8 25 ♘h6 mate.

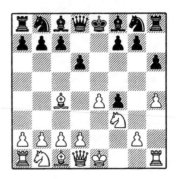

after 5 h4

after 11 ♕d3

after 18 ... ♗xf3

Sicilian: 3 ♘ge2
Kudrin-Fedorowicz
Ontario 1998

1 e4 c5 2 ♘c3 ♘c6 3 ♘ge2

An occasional favourite of Fischer and Spassky who liked to keep their opponents guessing whether the follow-up would be the usual d2-d4 or else g2-g3 with a Closed Sicilian.

3 ... e5

Fedorowicz puts a stop to the debate but the text runs the risk of losing control of the d5 square.

4 ♘d5 d6 5 ♘ec3 a6

Instead:

a) 5 ... ♘ge7 6 ♗c4 ♘xd5 7 ♘xd5 ♗e7 8 0-0 0-0 9 d3 ♗g5 10 ♕h5 ♗xc1 11 ♖axc1 ♘e7 12 f4 ♘xd5 13 ♗xd5 exf4 14 ♖xf4 ♗e6 ½-½ Tischbierek-Oll, New York 1994.

b) 5 ... ♗e6 6 ♗c4 ♗e7 7 0-0 ♘f6 8 d3 0-0 9 f4 exf4 10 ♗xf4 ♘xd5 11 ♘xd5 ♗xd5 12 ♗xd5 ♗f6 13 c3 and White's pair of bishops promise a small edge, Del Campo-Gonzalez, Cuba 1997.

6 a4 g6 7 ♗c4 ♗g7 8 d3 ♘h6 9 h4 f6 10 ♘xf6+!

This surprising sacrifice is part of a deep attacking plan which is easy to play and difficult to resist.

10 ... ♕xf6 11 ♗g5 ♕f8 12 ♘d5 ♘g4

Upon 12 ... ♗g4 White can maintain an advantage with 13 f3 ♗xf3 14 gxf3 ♖c8 15 0-0 intending f4.

13 0-0 ♘f6 14 ♘c7+ ♔e7 15 f4!

Unfortunately for Fedorowicz his position is rapidly deteriorating.

15 ... h6 16 ♗xf6+ ♗xf6 17 fxe5 ♘xe5 18 ♘d5+ ♔d7 19 ♖xf6 ♕g7 20 ♕d2 b6 21 ♖af1 ♖b8 22 ♘e3 ♖h7 23 d4 1-0

after 5 ♘ec3

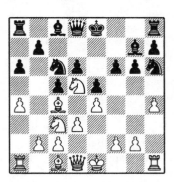

after 9 ... f6

after 15 f4

Chigorin: 4 cxd5
Svendsen-Reefschlaeger
Gausdal 1995

1 d4 d5 2 c4 ♘c6 3 ♘f3 ♗g4 4 cxd5

4 ♘c3 is a familiar sight but the text offers White a chance to avoid a main line.

4 ... ♗xf3 5 exf3?

This leads to disaster due to the weakness of the d4 pawn. Also possible are:

a) 5 dxc6 ♗xc6 6 ♘c3 ♘f6 7 f3 e6 8 e4 ♗e7 9 ♗e3 0-0 10 ♕d2 a6 11 ♗d3 b5 12 0-0 ♕d7+= Petran-Jakubek, Slovak 1996.

b) 5 gxf3 ♕xd5 6 e3 e6 7 ♘c3 ♕h5 8 f4 ♕xd1+ 9 ♔xd1 0-0-0 10 ♔e2 ♘f6 11 ♗g2 ♘e7 12 ♗d2 ♘f5 13 ♖hc1 ♔b8 14 a4 h6 15 ♘b5 ♖d7= Verat-Atalik, Cappelle la Grande 1995.

5 ... ♕xd5 6 ♗e3

It is possible to gambit the pawn with 6 ♘c3 but Black should be able to cope with the temporary pressure. For example: 6 ... ♕xd4 7 ♕c2 ♕d7 8 ♗b5 a6 9 ♗a4 e5 10 ♗e3 ♗d6 11 ♘e4 ♘ge7 12 ♘c5 ♕c8 13 h4 0-0 14 g4 ♘d5 15 ♗xc6 bxc6 16 ♘e4 f5 17 gxf5 ♕xf5 and Black is clearly better, Moutousis-Atalik, Peristeri 1994.

6 ... . 0-0-0 7 ♘c3 ♕a5 8 ♗b5

The pin on the d-file should dictate 8 ♕b3 when 8 ... e6 9 0-0-0 ♘f6 10 ♗c4 ♘b4 maintains an edge for Black.

8 ... ♘xd4! 9 ♗xd4 e5 10 ♕c2 exd4 11 ♕f5+ ♔b8 12 0-0-0 ♘h6 13 ♕f4 ♗a3!

The position is already overwhelming but this is a classy way to finish.

14 bxa3 ♕xa3+ 15 ♔b1 dxc3 0-1

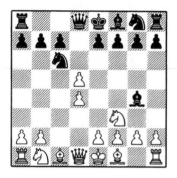

after 4 cxd5

after 8 ♗b5

after 13 ♕f4

English: 3 ... f5
Uhlmann-Dunnington
Zillertal 1993

1 c4 e5 2 ♘c3 d6 3 ♘f3 f5

An aggressive system which can transpose to various systems such as the reversed Closed Sicilian after ... ♘c6, ... g6, ... ♗g7 and ... ♘f6.

4 d4

a) 4 d3 ♘f6 5 ♗g5 c6 6 e3 ♘a6 7 ♗e2 ♘c7 8 b4 ♗e7 9 ♕b3 h6 10 ♗xf6 ♗xf6 11 ♖b1 0-0 12 0-0= R. Boulier-Dunnington, Lyon, 1990.

b) 4 e4 ♘f6 5 d3 ♘c6 6 ♗e2 g6 7 0-0 ♗g7 8 ♘d5 h6 9 ♗d2 a5 10 a3 g5 11 ♗c3 a4 12 ♘xf6+ ♕xf6 13 exf5 ♗xf5 14 ♘d2 0-0 15 ♘e4 ♕e7= Iglesias-Urday, Candas 1992.

c) 4 e3 ♘f6 5 ♗e2 c6 6 b4 ♗e7 7 ♗b2 0-0 8 0-0 ♔h8 9 b5 e4 10 ♘g5 ♕e8 11 d3 h6 12 ♘h3 ♘bd7 13 ♘f4 ♘e5= Panno-Rubinetti, Mar del Plata 1971.

4 ... e4 5 ♗g5 ♗e7 6 ♗xe7 ♕xe7 7 ♘d2 ♘f6 8 e3 0-0 9 ♗e2 c5 10 ♘b3 b6

Dunnington has time to make his pawn structure rock-solid because the closed nature of the position reduces the significance of his relative lack of development.

11 ♕d2 ♗b7 12 0-0-0 ♘c6 13 f4 exf3 14 ♗xf3 ♔h8 15 ♖he1 ♘e4 16 ♗xe4 fxe4 17 ♘d5 ♕f7 18 ♕e2 ♗a6

Pinpointing Black's weak c-pawn and, into the bargain, threatening in some lines ... ♕xd5.

19 ♕c2

On 19 ♘d2 then 19 ... ♗xc4! 20 ♕xc4 ♘a5 21 ♕c2 ♕xd5 wins.

19 ... cxd4 20 exd4 b5 21 cxb5 ♕xd5 22 bxc6 ♖ac8 23 ♔b1 ♖xc6 24 ♕d2 ♗d3+ 25 ♔a1 ♕xb3! 0-1

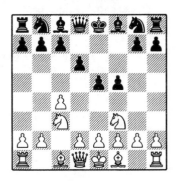

after 3 ... f5

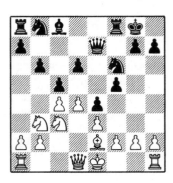

after 10 ... b6

after 25 ♔a1

Scotch: 7 ♗c4
Kupreichik-Romanishin
USSR Championship 1976

1 e4 e5 2 ♘f3 ♘c6 3 d4 exd4 4 ♘xd4 ♗c5 5 ♗e3 ♕f6 6 c3 ♘ge7 7 ♗b5

This system has been largely forgotten since Kasparov set a new trend with 7 ♗c4.

7 ... d6

a) 7 ... ♗b6 8 0-0 0-0 9 ♕d2 ♕g6 10 ♖e1 ♘e5 11 ♔h1 d5 (11 ... d6!?) 12 ♗f4 ♘g4 13 f3 ♘f6 14 e5 ½-½ Fodre-Flear, Paris 1990.

b) 7 ... a6 8 ♗a4 b5 9 ♗c2 0-0 10 0-0 ♘e5 11 ♘d2 d5 12 f3 ♗d7 13 ♗f2 ♕g5 14 ♔h1 ♘5g6 15 exd5 ♗xd4 16 ♗xd4 ♘xd5 17 ♘e4 ♕h6 18 ♗xg7 ♕xg7 19 ♕xd5+– Chorvatova-Ostojic, Mureck 1998

8 0-0 0-0 9 ♘xc6?!

The resulting position is easy for Black to play so I would suggest 9 f4!? as a possible improvement.

9 ... bxc6 10 ♗xc5 cxb5 11 ♗d4 ♕g6 12 ♘d2 c5 13 ♗e3 f5!

Romanishin is quick to try and exchange the central pawn because he wants to open up the a8-h1 diagonal for his bishop.

14 ♕f3

14 f3 is met by 14 ... f4 15 ♗f2 ♗h3 16 ♗g3 fxg3 17 gxh3∓.

14 ... ♗d7!

A slight change of plan is called for, otherwise 14 ... ♗b7? 15 exf5! is embarrassing for Black.

15 ♖fe1 ♖ae8 16 exf5 ♘xf5 17 ♕d5+ ♗e6 18 ♕d3 c4!

Romanishin has found a way for his bishop to gain access to the long diagonal which spells trouble for White in defending g2.

19 ♕f1 ♗d5 20 ♗xa7 ♘h4 21 g3 ♕f7 22 ♖xe8 ♘f3+ 0-1

after 7 ♗b5

after 13 ♗e3

after 22 ... ♘f3+

Pirc: 5 ♗e3
Carlier-Kerkhof
Brussels 1995

1 ♘f3 g6 2 e4 ♗g7 3 d4 d6 4 ♘c3 ♘f6 5 ♗e3 0-0

Carlier-Bernard, Brussels 1995, went instead 5 ... c6 6 ♕d2 b5 7 ♗d3 ♘bd7 8 0-0 0-0 9 ♗h6 b4 10 ♘e2 c5 11 ♗xg7 ♔xg7 12 e5 (note the similarity to the main game) 12 ... ♘e8 13 dxc5 dxc5 14 ♗e4 ♖b8 15 ♘g3 ♘c7 16 ♘h5+ ♔h8 17 ♕h6 1-0.

6 ♕d2

White adopts a modern set-up which indicates a willingness to castle queenside, play ♗h6 to exchange dark-squared bishops and then start a kingside attack.

6 ... ♘a6?!

Practice has also seen:

a) 6 ... a6 7 ♗h6 b5 8 ♗xg7 ♔xg7 9 ♗d3 ♗b7 10 e5 ♘fd7 11 h4 dxe5 12 h5 ♖h8 13 0-0-0 exd4 14 ♗e4 and White stood better in Johansen-Reilly, Melbourne 1998.

b) 6 ... ♗g4 7 ♘g5 a6 (7 ... c6!?) 8 f3 ♗c8 9 h4 e6 10 h5 h6 11 ♘h3 g5 12 ♘xg5 hxg5 13 h6 ♗h8 14 ♗xg5 ♕d7 15 ♕f4 ♘h7 16 ♕g3 f5 17 ♗f6+ ♔f7 18 ♗xh8 1-0 Kogan-Reinderman, Antwerp 1998.

7 0-0-0 ♘g4 8 ♗g5 c5 9 h3 ♘f6 10 e5 cxd4 11 ♕xd4 ♘d7 12 ♕h4

The opening has been a triumph for White. The pressure on e7 forces Black to make further concessions which fatally undermine his defence.

12 ... f6 13 ♗c4+ ♔h8 14 exf6 ♘xf6 15 ♗h6 ♘c5 16 ♘g5 e6 17 ♖he1 d5 18 ♗xd5!

An excellent riposte.

18 ... exd5 19 ♘xd5 1-0

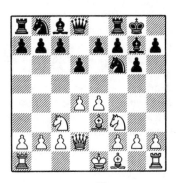

after 6 ♕d2

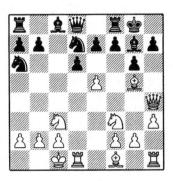

after 12 ♕h4

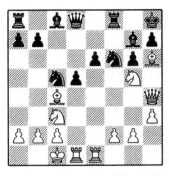

after 17 ... d5

Nimzowitsch: 5 ♗e3
Binham-Horn
Bonnevoie 1998

1 e4 ♘c6 2 ♘c3 ♘f6 3 d4 d6 4 ♘f3 ♗g4

Horn adopts a flexible line where Black can counter in the centre with ... e6 and ... d5 or even exchange on f3 and follow with ... g6 entering a position similar to the Pirc.

5 ♗e3 a6

A sneaky move which stops the troublesome ♗b5 but is rather slow.

a) 5 ... e6 6 ♗e3 ♗e7 7 d5 exd5 8 exd5 ♗xf3 9 ♗xf3 ♘e5 10 ♗e2 0-0 11 f4 ♘ed7 12 ♗f3 ♖e8 13 ♕d2 ♘c5 14 0-0-0 a5 15 g4 a4 16 g5 ♘fd7 17 h4 ♘b6 18 ♗d4 ♗f8 19 ♖he1 ½-½ Rohl-Rogers, New York 1998.

b) 5 ... e5 6 ♗b5 ♘d7 7 d5 ♘cb8 8 ♗e2 ♗e7 9 ♕d2 h6 10 0-0-0 ♗xf3 11 gxf3 a6 12 f4+= Sveshnikov-Mestrovic, Ljubljana 1994.

6 ♗e2 e6 7 0-0 ♗e7 8 h3 ♗h5 9 d5 exd5 10 exd5 ♘b8

10 ... ♘e5?! is no good as 11 ♘xe5 ♗xe2 12 ♘xf7! ♗xd1 13 ♘xd8 ♗xc2 14 ♘e6 leaves Black facing the loss of a pawn.

11 ♘d4 ♗g6 12 f4 ♗e4 13 ♘xe4 ♘xe4 14 ♗f3 ♘f6 15 ♘f5

The perfect square for the knight to dominate the game—made possible by the relentless pursuit of Black's light-squared bishop.

15 ... 0-0 16 ♗d4 ♖e8 17 ♕e1 ♘bd7 18 ♕g3 g6 19 ♘h6+ ♔f8 20 f5 ♘e5 21 ♖ae1 ♘h5 22 ♗xh5 ♗h4 23 fxg6!!

Amazingly, the queen is given up for a stylish checkmate.

23 ... ♗xg3 24 ♖xf7+ 1-0

24 ... ♘xf7 25 g7 mate.

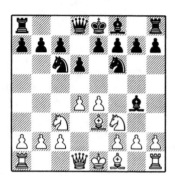

after 5 ♗e3

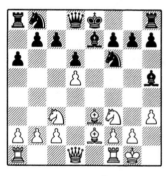

after 10 ... ♘b8

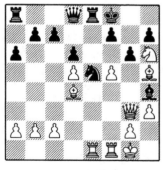

after 22 ... ♗h4

Dutch: 4 ... c5
Averbakh-Goldberg
USSR Championship 1950

**1 d4 e6 2 ♘f3 f5 3 g3 ♘f6 4 ♗g2
c5**

An unusual line to avoid theory.

5 c4

a) 5 0-0 ♘c6 6 c4 cxd4 7 ♘xd4
♗e7 8 ♘c3 0-0 9 b3 ♘g4 10 ♘xc6
dxc6 11 h3 ♘f6 12 ♕xd8 ♖xd8 13
♗e3 e5= Berger-Keres, Margate
1937

b) 5 c3 cxd4 6 cxd4 ♗b4+ 7 ♗d2
♕b6 8 ♕b3 ♘c6 9 0-0 ♘e4 10
♗xb4 ♕xb4 11 ♕xb4 ♘xb4 12
♘c3+= Markowski-Oliwa, Ringsted
1992.

5 ... cxd4 6 ♘xd4 ♗e7 7 ♘c3 a6

A prelude to attacking the c-pawn
with ... ♕c7 but 7 ... ♘c6 is better
transposing to note 'a' above.

8 0-0 ♕c7 9 e4! g6?

This fails to a tactical trick so 9 ...
fxe4 is a better try when 10 ♕e2
preserves a small advantage.

10 exf5 gxf5 11 ♘xf5!

The tell-tale signs of a lack of development and a stranded king is
enough for Averbakh to make a
spectacular sacrifice.

11 ... exf5 12 ♖e1 d6

After 12 ... h6 an analysis by Averbakh concludes that White has a
winning attack: 13 ♗f4 ♕d8 (13 ...
♕xc4 14 ♖c1) 14 ♘d5 ♘xd5 15
♕h5+ ♔f8 16 ♗xd5.

13 ♗g5 ♔d8

There is little choice as 13 ... ♔f7
or 13 ... 0-0 is crushed by 14 ♘d5.

**14 ♖xe7 ♕xe7 15 ♘d5 ♘xd5 16
♗xe7+ ♘xe7 17 ♕xd6+ ♘d7 18
♖d1 ♖g8**

If 18 ... ♖a7 then 19 ♕b6+.

**19 ♗xb7 ♖g6 20 ♕d4 ♘c6 21
♕b6+ ♔e8 22 ♗xc6 1-0**

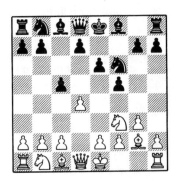

after 4 ... c5

after 10 ... gxf5

after 13 ... ♔d8

Caro-Kann: 4 ... ♘d7
Watson-Meduna
Prague 1992

1 e4 c6 2 d4 d5 3 ♘d2 dxe4 4 ♘xe4 ♘d7 5 ♘g5 ♘gf6 6 ♗d3

This formation is White's most aggressive option.

6 ... g6!?

A minor line compared to the main alternative 6 ... e6. A celebrated game indicates that Black has to be wary: 7 ♘1f3 h6? (7 ... ♗e7 or 7 ... ♗d6 are more acceptable) 8 ♘xe6! ♕e7 9 0-0 fxe6 10 ♗g6+ ♔d8 11 ♗f4 b5 12 a4 ♗b7 13 ♖e1 ♘d5 14 ♗g3 ♔c8 15 axb5 cxb5 16 ♕d3 ♗c6 17 ♗f5 exf5 18 ♖xe7 ♗xe7 19 c4 1-0 Deep Blue-Kasparov, New York 1997.

7 ♘1f3 ♗g7 8 ♕e2! 0-0

8 ... h6 is a calculated gamble by Black to survive the attack and end up with an extra piece. 9 ♘e6 (9 ♘e4!?) fxe6 10 ♕xe6+ ♔f8 11 ♗d2 ♘b6 12 0-0-0 ♗d7 13 ♔b1 ♗e8 14 ♘e5 gives White good attacking opportunities.

9 h4 h6 10 h5!

A touch of brilliance. Watson pulls out all the stops to open the h-file and accelerate the onslaught.

10 ... ♘xh5

The critical test is 10 ... hxg5 snatching the piece 11 h6! ♗h8 12 ♘xg5 ♘b6 13 h7+ ♔g7 14 ♕d2! intending ♘e6+ gives White an immense attack.

11 g4 ♘hf6 12 ♘e6! fxe6 13 ♕xe6+ ♖f7 14 ♗xg6 ♕f8 15 g5 ♘d5 16 gxh6 ♘e5 17 ♗h7+! 1-0

If 17 ... ♔xh7 (17 ... ♔h8 18 hxg7+ ♕xg7 19 ♗e4+ ♔g8 20 ♕xe5+-) 18 hxg7+ ♔xg7 19 ♕h6+ ♔g8 20 ♕h8 mate.

after 6 ... g6

after 9 ... h6

after 17 ♗h7+

Giuoco Piano: 5 d3
Bolzoni-Lane
Belgian Team Championship 1998

1 e4 e5 2 ♘f3 ♘c6 3 ♗c4 ♗c5 4 0-0 ♘f6 5 d3

The closed version of the Giuoco Piano gives priority to development and commencement of active operations only in the middlegame.

5 ... d6 6 c3 a6 7 b4 ♗a7

The point of my sixth move is revealed. After a standard reply such as 6 ... 0-0 then 7 b4 ♗b6 8 a4 a6 9 a5 ♗a7 10 b5 reaches a position similar to the game except that White has gained time by the forced retreat of the black bishop.

8 b5 ♘a5!

A surprise to the Belgian international who expected 8 ... axb5 9 ♗xb5 with equal chances.

9 bxa6 ♘xc4 10 axb7 ♗xb7 11 ♕a4+ ♕d7 12 ♕xc4

Consistent, especially as the ending 12 ♕xd7+ offers White nothing due to the weak doubled c-pawns: After 12 ... ♘xd7 13 dxc4 ♗xe4 14 ♘bd2 ♗d3 15 ♖e1 ♗b6 intending ... ♖a4 wins.

12 ... ♗a6!

The move that blows a hole in White's plans, because 13 ♕xa6 loses to 13 ... ♗xf2+.

13 ♕b4

There is no good square for the queen, e.g. 13 ♕b3 ♗xd3 14 ♖d1 ♖b8 (14 ... ♘xe4 also looks good 15 ♖xd3 ♘xf2 16 ♖e3 ♘g4 17 c4 e4 18 ♘e1 ♕f5-+) 15 ♖xd3 ♖xb3 16 axb3 ♕b5 17 c4 ♕b7 wins.

13 ... ♗xd3 14 ♖e1 ♖b8 15 ♕a3 ♗c5 16 ♘xe5 ♕e6! 17 ♕xc5 dxc5 18 ♘xd3 c4 19 ♘b2 ♘g4 20 h3 ♘e5 21 ♖e3 0-0 22 ♘d2 ♖fd8 23 f4 ♖xb2 0-1

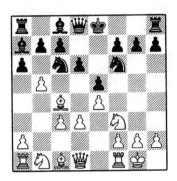

after 8 b5

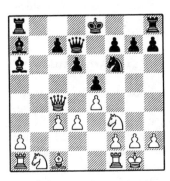

after 12 ... ♗a6

after 16 ♘xe5

Conclusion

The thrill of playing a scintillating move has to be tempered with the knowledge that the right position has to be achieved first! In most cases a carefully considered plan was a prerequisite to the construction of a formidable attack. In Watson-Meduna, White followed a main line but was able to introduce an original and aggressive sequence as soon as Black deviated. Though the game ends in some spectacular fireworks, also present are familiar factors such as weakening of the defensive pawn shield and rapid deployment of reinforcements for the attack.

The Art of Attack

1 Look for typical motifs. In a position arising from a Pirc such as in Carlier-Kerhoff, White is eager to exchange dark-squared bishops to weaken the defence and aim for the advance e4-e5 ousting the defensive knight on f6. This lays the foundations for a winning move.

2 Punish quickly any unusual opening which neglects development. In Averbakh-Goldberg, White gave Black no time to consolidate and jumped at the chance to hold the black king in the centre, thus allowing his attack to rage on.

3 Do not underestimate the importance of psychology. When a player comes under relentless pressure from an attack then something is likely to give. This is usually the moment when a star move makes its appearance.

The Art of Defence

1 Gain a good knowledge of typical traps so these can be spotted in advance.

2 Familiarise yourself with basic opening ideas. Taking on, say, the King's Gambit or a main line Open Sicilian with only a little knowledge is asking for trouble.

3 Develop your pieces. This simple principle, repeated over and again throughout this book, cannot be disregarded and is a contributory factor to so many defeats.

7 Opening to the Ending

When we discuss the 'attack' we immediately think of a queen being involved in some mating combination in the opening or middlegame. However, any assumption that tactics are unlikely because queens have been exchanged is wrong and can lead to complacency—with disastrous consequences. Never forget that the ending too can offer many opportunities for a player on the look-out for a decisive blow.

The Spanish Exchange is one of the best known ways to secure an early queen-swap and its various possibilities are examined in the game Fischer-Spassky. The American was renowned for using this opening and his games are a guiding light to others who wish to create mating attacks.

If there is one thing that King's Indian players hate it is the thought that their prepared aggressive variation can be thwarted by the Exchange Variation—with both queens leaving the board after just eight moves. In the game, Ryba-Hillarp Persson, Black reminds us that there is no need to shake hands for an early draw and gradually increases the pressure by improving the positions of his pieces. No easy victory but plenty to battle for.

In Luther-Maiwald, Black follows basic principles by castling early and fending off the initial offensive —and all seems fine. However, a close scrutiny of the game reveals that Black has problems with his passively placed pieces which allow his opponent to make rapid progress with an attack. It's a similar story in Miles-A.Rodriguez.

In Adams-Lautier, White starts off with aggressive intent—which is by no means reduced by the time the ending is reached. This game is a model example of how to place obstacles in your opponent's way and wait for him to trip up.

Seeking complications in an attempt to avoid drawing lines at all cost is another way a player can get into a mess. This is the case in Lane-Nunn where Black embarks on a king advance in the search for attacking chances, only to end up being mated himself!

It seems too good to be true to be able to swap queens, sacrifice and then checkmate—but that is exactly what happened in Doubleday-South. The roots of White's demise lay in his kingside pieces being rooted to their original squares while Black focused on the attack.

A surprise opening move, such as that seen in Epishin-Komarov, can lead a defender to unfamiliar territory which inevitably makes the game more difficult for him. Here, as the game rapidly approaches the ending, White's pieces take control of all the most important squares and dominate the board.

Remember, no matter how few pieces remain, the endgame demands accurate play and the need to be ever alert to tactical tricks.

Grunfeld: 4 ♗f4
Chekhov-Krasilnikov
Moscow 1998

1 d4 ♘f6 2 c4 g6 3 ♘c3 d5 4 ♗f4

A positional continuation which has been employed by Capablanca and Karpov. The bishop exerts pressure on the h2-b8 diagonal.

4 ... ♗g7 5 e3 c5 6 dxc5 ♕a5 7 ♕a4+

White is happy to enter the ending because Black has to overcome various obstacles to regain his pawn.

7 ... ♕xa4 8 ♘xa4 ♘e4

a) 8 ... ♗e6?! 9 ♗xb8 ♖xb8 10 cxd5 ♘xd5?! (10 ... ♗xd5 11 ♗b5+ ♗c6 12 ♗xc6 bxc6 13 ♖d1+=) 11 ♗b5+ ♔d8 12 ♖c1! a6 13 ♗c4 ♘b4 14 ♗xe6 fxe6 15 ♖c4 ♘xa2 16 ♔e2± Dreev-Leko, Dortmund 1994.

b) 8 ... ♗d7 9 ♘c3 ♘e4 10 ♘xd5 ♘a6 11 f3 ♘exc5 12 ♖b1! e6 13 ♘c7+ ♘xc7 14 ♗xc7 ♘a4 15 ♗d6 += Novikov-Kudrin, Toronto 1998.

9 cxd5 ♗d7 10 f3 ♗xa4 11 fxe4 ♗xb2 12 ♖b1 ♗c3+ 13 ♔f2 ♘d7 14 ♖c1 ♘xc5 15 ♔f3

The bishop is taboo: 15 ♖xc3? ♘xe4+ 16 ♔f3 ♘xc3 17 ♗e5 ♗d1+! 18 ♔g3 ♘e4+ 19 ♔f4 ♘f2 and now Black is winning.

15 ... ♗b4 16 ♖c4 ♗b5 17 ♖xb4 ♗xf1 18 ♘e2 ♗xe2+ 19 ♔xe2 ♔d7

He should not centralise the king with enemy men swarming around.

20 e5 h6?! 21 e4 ♖ac8 22 ♗e3 b6

22 ... a5 23 ♖b5 ♘xe4 24 ♔d3 f5 25 ♖xb7+ wins.

23 ♖f1 ♖h7 24 ♖c4 ♘b7?

Black is in trouble but this hastens his demise. 24 ... h5 25 ♖fc1 h4 26 ♗xc5 bxc5 27 ♖xc5±

25 e6+! 1-0

Black resigned in view of 25 ... fxe6 26 dxe6+ ♔d8 27 ♖f8 mate.

after 4 ♗f4

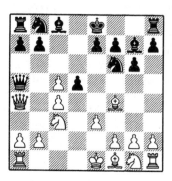

after 7 ♕a4+

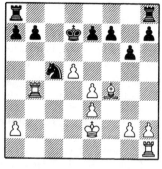

after 19 ... ♔d7

Grand Prix Attack: 2 ... e6
Adams-Lautier
Tilburg 1997

1 e4 c5 2 ♘c3 e6 3 f4
The Grand Prix Attack.
3 ... d5 4 ♘f3 dxe4
A quiet line to avoid White's usual attacking formation. Instead:

a) 4 ... d4 5 ♘e2 ♘f6 6 ♘g3 ♘c6 7 ♗b5 ♗d7 8 0-0 ♗e7 9 d3 a6 10 ♗xc6 ♗xc6 11 f5+= Nogradi-Szabo, Hungary 1994.

b) 4 ... ♘f6 5 ♗b5+ ♗d7 6 ♗xd7+ ♕xd7 7 ♘e5 ♕c7 8 exd5 exd5 9 ♕f3 d4 (9 ... ♗d6 10 0-0 ♘c6 11 ♘g4+= Lane-Lacklison, Brussels 1998) 10 ♘b5 ♕e7 11 ♔d1! (this new move changes the assessment of the line heavily in White's favour) 11 ... ♘a6 12 ♘c6! 1-0 Bhend-Rolli, Baden 1998.

5 ♘xe4 ♗e7 6 d4 cxd4 7 ♕xd4 ♕xd4 8 ♘xd4
The ending is roughly equal but White has a slight initiative thanks to the space advantage.

8 ... a6 9 ♗e3 ♘d7 10 g3 ♘gf6 11 ♗g2 ♘xe4 12 ♗xe4 ♘c5 13 ♗f3 ♗d7 14 0-0-0 ♖c8
14 ... 0-0-0 might be a better idea because the king can then defend the b-pawn.

15 ♖d2 ♖c7 16 ♖hd1 ♘a4 17 ♘e2 ♗b5 18 ♗d4 f6
The obvious 18 ... 0-0 is well met by 19 ♗e5 which wins a pawn.

19 b3!
The tactics favour Adams because the rook on c7 is overloaded with the defence of the b7 pawn.

19 ... ♗b4
Other moves do not help: 19 ... ♗xe2 20 ♖xe2 ♘c5 21 b4 or 19 ... ♘c5 20 ♗xc5 ♗xe2 21 ♖xe2 ♗xc5 22 ♗d5! both win for White.

20 bxa4 ♗xd2+ 21 ♖xd2 ♗xa4 22 ♘c3 ♗c6 23 ♗h5+ 1-0

after 4 ♘f3

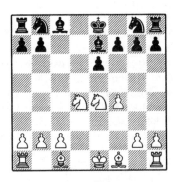

after 8 ♘xd4

after 19 b3

Spanish: Exchange Variation
Fischer-Spassky
Game Nine, Stefi Stefan 1992

1 e4 e5 2 ♘f3 ♘c6 3 ♗b5 a6 4 ♗xc6

This opening has been very popular ever since Bobby Fischer played it at the Havana Olympiad 1966. Often an ending arises straight after the opening where White tries to exploit his kingside pawn advantage.

4 ... dxc6 5 0-0 f6 6 d4 exd4 7 ♘xd4 c5

a) 7 ... ♗c5?? (played numerous times) 8 ♕h5+ 1-0 Dantas-Petersen, Zagan 1995.

b) 7 ... ♕d6!? 8 ♗e3 ♗d7 9 ♘d2 c5 10 ♘4b3 b6 11 a4 a5 12 ♕f3 ♘e7 13 ♖fd1 ♘g6? 14 e5 ♕c6 15 e6! 1-0 Kolcak-Sarkosy, Swedish Team Championship 1994

8 ♘b3 ♕xd1 9 ♖xd1 ♗g4 10 f3 ♗e6 11 ♘c3 ♗d6 12 ♗e3 b6 13 a4 0-0-0?!

13 ... ♔f7 looks better, e.g. 14 a5 c4 15 ♘d4 b5 16 ♘xe6 ♔xe6=.

14 a5 ♔b7 15 e5 ♗e7

After 15 ... fxe5? 16 axb6 cxb6 17 ♘e4 ♗e7 18 ♖xd8 ♗xd8 19 ♘bxc5+ White wins material.

16 ♖xd8 ♗xd8 17 ♘e4! ♔c6?

Spassky walks into a clever trap.

After 17 ... ♗xb3 18 cxb3 ♘e7 19 axb6 cxb6 20 exf6 (20 ♘d6+?! ♔c6 21 ♖xa6 ♘d5=) 20 ... gxf6 21 ♖d1 ♘f5 22 ♗f2 White is slightly better.

18 axb6 cxb6 19 ♘bxc5!

A glorious move.

19 ... ♗c8

19 ... bxc5 20 ♖xa6+ ♗b6 21 ♗xc5+-.

20 ♘xa6 fxe5 21 ♘b4+ 1-0

Because of 21 ... ♔b5 22 ♘d6+ ♔xb4 23 ♖a3 intending c3 mate.

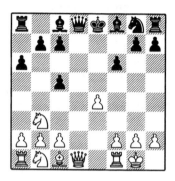

after 8 ♘b3

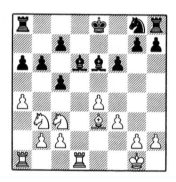

after 13 a4

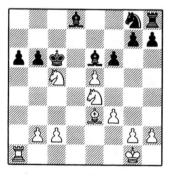

after 19 ♘bxc5

Slav: 6 ♕b3
Hebden-Crouch
British League (4NCL) 1998

1 d4 d5 2 c4 c6 3 ♘f3 ♘f6 4 e3 ♗f5 5 cxd5

A forcing line which avoids the complications of 5 ♗d3.

5 ... cxd5 6 ♕b3 ♕b6

Black enters an ending with weak doubled b-pawns as he has compensation in the half-open a-file.

a) 7 ... ♕c8 7 ♗d2 ♘c6 8 ♗b5 e6 9 0-0 ♗d6 10 ♗b4 ♕c7 11 ♕a3 ♗xb4 12 ♕xb4 ♕e7 13 ♗xc6+ bxc6 14 ♕xe7+ ♔xe7 15 ♘e5 ♖hc8 16 ♖c1 ♘d7 17 ♘xc6+ ♔d6 18 ♘a3! was played in Benjamin-Christiansen, USA Champ. 1997.

b) 6 ... ♕c7 7 ♘c3 e6 8 ♗d2 ♘c6 9 ♖c1 ♗e7 10 ♘e5 0-0 11 ♗b5 ♖fc8 (11 ... ♘xe5 12 ♘xd5 ♕xc1+ 13 ♗xc1 ♘xd5 14 e4! is better for White) 12 ♘a4 ♘e4 13 ♗xc6 ♘xd2 14 ♔xd2 bxc6 15 ♘xc6+- Ricardi-Cativelli, Clarin 1997.

7 ♕xb6 axb6 8 ♘c3 e6 9 ♗b5+ ♘fd7 10 ♘e5 ♗d6 11 ♘xd7 ♘xd7 12 ♗d2

The pin on the knight is awkward.

12 ... ♔d8?!

Better is 12 ... ♔e7 to co-ordinate the rooks when, after 13 0-0 ♘f6 14 f3, White can aim for e3-e4. In Hebden-Beikert, Cappelle la Grande 1992, Black prepared to double rooks on the a-file with 12 ... ♖a5 13 ♔e2 ♔e7 14 ♖hc1 h5 15 h3 ♘f6, when White again played 16 f3 to take control of the centre.

13 0-0 ♘f6 14 f3 ♗g6 15 ♖fc1 ♘e8 16 ♘a4 ♗c7 17 ♗b4 f5?!

17 ... f6 is a better bet.

18 f4 ♗h5 19 ♖c2 g5 20 fxg5 h6 21 g6 ♗xg6 22 ♗e1 f4 23 ♘xb6!
1-0

after 6 ♕b3

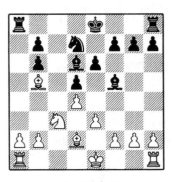

after 12 ♗d2

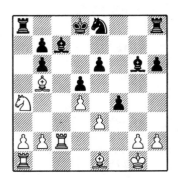

after 22 ... f4

Closed Sicilian: 2 ... e6
Lane-Nunn
Stroud 1980

1 e4 c5 2 ♘c3 e6 3 g3 d5 4 exd5 exd5 5 d4 cxd4 6 ♕xd4 ♘f6

In Lane-Bologan, Cappelle la Grande 1992, my opponent concentrated on defending the isolated d-pawn which allowed me to create a winning attack: 6 ... ♗e6 7 ♗g2 ♘c6 8 ♕a4 ♗b4 9 ♘ge2 a6 10 0-0 ♘ge7 11 ♘f4 0-0 12 ♘ce2 ♗c5 13 c3 b5 14 ♕d1 ♗b6 15 a4 b4 16 cxb4 ♘xb4 17 b3 ♖c8 18 ♗b2 ♗f5 19 ♘d4 ♗e4 20 ♕g4! ♘g6 21 ♗xe4 dxe4 22 ♘f5 ♖c5 23 ♘h5+-.

7 ♗g5 ♗e7 8 ♗b5+ ♘c6 9 ♗xf6 ♗xf6 10 ♕c5

This crafty move prevents castling, puts pressure on the knight at c6 and invites Black to enter an ending. It sounds great but before this game it was not widely known that one could transpose into the obscure reversed Goring Gambit Declined! This position arises after the move-order 1 e4 e5 2 ♘f3 ♘c6 3 d4 exd4 4 c3 d5 5 exd5 ♕xd5 6 cxd4 ♗g4 7 ♗e2 ♗b4+ 8 ♘c3 ♗xf3 9 ♗xf3 ♕c4. The only difference is that White has added g3 and the resulting endgame should still be equal.

10 ... ♗xc3+ 11 bxc3 ♕e7+ 12 ♕xe7+ ♔xe7 13 0-0-0 ♗e6 14 ♘e2 ♔d6 15 ♖he1 ♔c5 16 c4 dxc4 17 ♗xc6 bxc6?

The grandmaster prefers to maintain the tension and wrongly avoids 17 ... ♔xc6 18 ♘d4+ ♔c7 19 ♘xe6+ fxe6 20 ♖xe6 ♖he8=.

18 ♘f4 ♗g4 19 ♖e5+ ♔b4 20 ♖d4 ♗e6 21 a3+! ♔xa3

21 ... ♔c3 22 ♖d6 ♗g4 23 ♖e3 mate.

22 ♘xe6 ♔b4 23 ♖c5 1-0

after 5 d4

after 10 ♕c5

after 20 ... ♗e6

English Opening: 7 ♕f5
Miles-Rodriguez
Yopal 1997

1 c4 ♘f6 2 ♘c3 e5 3 ♘f3 ♘c6 4 e3 ♗b4 5 ♕c2 0-0 6 ♘d5 ♖e8 7 ♕f5

An idea of Michael Stean to inconvenience Black at an early stage of the game with the threat 8 ♘g5.

7 ... d6

a) 7 ... ♗f8? 8 ♘g5 and the threat of ♘xf6+ followed by ♕xh7+ leaves Black busted.

b) 7 ... ♗e7?! 8 ♘xe5 ♘b4 9 ♘xb4 ♗xb4 10 a3!? d5?! (10 ... d6!?) 11 ♕c2 ♖xe5 12 axb4 ♗f5 13 d3 ♕e7 14 ♗d2 d4 15 ♗e2 dxe3 16 fxe3 ♗g4 17 ♗f3!± Kasparov-Romanishin, USSR Champ 1978.

c) 7 ... ♘xd5? 8 cxd5 d6 9 ♕e4 ♘d4 10 ♘xd4 exd4 11 ♕xd4± Rayner-Clarke, Dublin 1993.

8 ♘xf6+ ♕xf6

After 8 ... gxf6 9 ♕h5 Black's king is exposed to danger but this has the merit of creating a double-edged game. For example 9 ... e4 10 a3 ♗c5 11 b4 ♗b6 12 ♘h4 a5 13 b5 ♘e5 14 f4 ♘g6 15 ♗b2+= Logothetis-Skembris, Athens 1997.

9 ♕xf6 gxf6 10 a3 ♗c5 11 b4 ♗b6 12 ♗b2 a5 13 b5 ♘e7 14 d4!? ♗g4?

Ribli underestimates the threat to smother the bishop on c5. 14 ... a4!? looks best to give the bishop an escape square. White can continue 15 0-0-0 with a slight space advantage.

15 c5! ♗a7 16 b6 ♗xf3 17 gxf3 ♗b8 18 ♖g1+ ♔f8 19 ♖d1!

Miles is clearly on top due to the passive position of the Black pieces.

19 ... c6 20 dxe5 fxe5 21 cxd6 ♘d5 22 e4 ♘xb6 23 f4! f6 24 fxe5 ♘d7 25 ♗c4 1-0

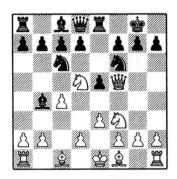

after 7 ♕f5

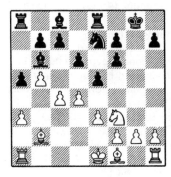

after 14 d4

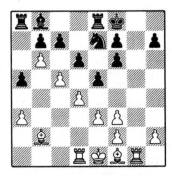

after 19 ♖d1

Queen's Indian: 5 ♕b3
Epishin-Komarov
St.Petersburg 1997

1 d4 ♘f6 2 c4 e6 3 ♘f3 b6 4 g3 ♗a6 5 ♕b3

Rare. 5 ♘bd2, Adorjan-Kudrin, is featured under 'Greedy Openings'.

5 ... c5

a) 5 ... d5 6 cxd5 exd5 7 ♗g5 ♗e7 8 ♘c3 ♗b7 9 ♗xf6 ♗xf6 10 ♗g2 0-0 11 0-0 ♖e8 12 ♖fe1 ♘a6 13 ♖ad1 ♕d6 14 ♕a4+= Grivas-Kalesis, Budapest 1994.

b) 5 ... ♘c6 6 ♘bd2 ♘a5 7 ♕a4 ♗b7 8 ♗g2 c5 9 dxc5 bxc5 10 0-0 ♗e7 11 ♘e5 ♗xg2 12 ♔xg2 0-0 13 ♘df3 d6 14 ♗d2 dxe5 15 ♗xa5 ♕b8 16 ♗c3+= Sorin-Almasi, Buenos Aires 1996

6 d5 exd5 7 cxd5 c4?!

A poor practical choice because the c-pawn is a long-term weakness. The game Peric-Epishin, Geneva 1997, went instead 7 ... g6 8 ♗f4 d6 9 ♗g2 ♗g7 10 ♕e3+ ♔f8 11 ♘c3 h6 12 ♕c1 ♕e7 13 0-0 ♘bd7 14 h3 ♖e8 15 a4 with a draw.

8 ♕e3+ ♕e7 9 ♘c3 ♕xe3 10 ♗xe3 ♗b4 11 ♗d4!

Epishin has a lot of pressure and the tactics are in his favour.

11 ... ♘xd5

After 11 ... ♔e7 12 0-0-0 Black is also in trouble:

a) 12 ... ♖e8 13 d6+! ♗xd6 14 ♗xf6+ gxf6 15 ♘d5+ ♔d8 16 ♘xf6 ♖e6 17 ♘xh7+-.

b) 12 ... d6 13 e4 ♘bd7 14 ♘h4 g6 15 f4 ♖he8 16 e5 ♘g4 17 ♘f3 ±.

12 ♗xg7 ♖g8 13 0-0-0! ♘e7 14 ♗e5 ♘bc6 15 ♘e4 0-0-0 16 ♘d6+ ♗xd6 17 ♗xd6 ♖g6 18 ♖d2! ♘f5 19 ♗f4

Threatening to put a stranglehold on the position with ♗d6

19 ... ♗b7?! 20 e4 ♘b4 21 exf5 ♗xf3 22 fxg6 ♗xh1 23 gxf7 1-0

after 5 ♕b3

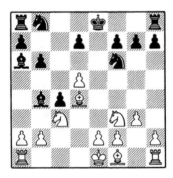

after 11 ♗d4

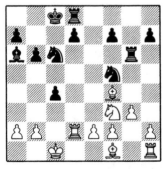

after 19 ♗f4

Queen's Gambit Declined: 4 ... c5
Doubleday-South
Ottawa Championship 1977

1 d4 d5 2 c4 e6 3 ♘c3 ♘f6 4 ♗g5 c5

Seeking less explored variations.

5 cxd5 cxd4!?

An idea of the Dutchman Prins.

6 ♕a4+!?

It is probably better to play 6 ♕xd4. Then 6 ... ♗e7 7 e4 ♘c6:

a) 8 ♗b5 0-0 9 ♗xc6 bxc6 10 ♗xf6 ♗xf6 11 e5 c5 12 ♕e3 exd5 13 ♘ge2 d4 14 ♕e4 ♗a6 15 ♘d5 ♗xe5 16 0-0 ♖e8 17 f4 ♗f6 18 ♕f5 ♗xe2 19 ♖fe1 d3 20 ♘xf6+ ♕xf6 0-1 Roods-Gross, Hawaii 1998.

b) 8 ♕d2 ♘xd5 9 exd5 ♗xg5 10 f4 ♗h4+ 11 g3 exd5 12 gxh4 ♕xh4+ 13 ♕f2 ♕e7+ 14 ♕e2 ♗e6 15 ♘f3 d4 16 ♘b5 0-0-0! 17 ♖c1 ♔b8 with compensation in Brinck Claussen-Pyhala, Espoo 1987.

6 ... ♕d7 7 ♕xd4

Or 7 dxe6? ♕xa4 8 exf7+ ♔xf7 9 ♘xa4 b5-+.

7 ... ♘c6 8 ♕a4 ♘xd5 9 0-0-0 ♗e7 10 ♗f4?!

a) 10 ♗xe7 ♘xc3! 11 bxc3 ♕xe7=+.

b) 10 ♗d2 0-0 11 ♘f3 a6! 12 e3 ♘db4 13 ♘e4 b5 14 ♕a3 ♕c7=+ Engqvist-Pedersen, Oslo 1992.

10 ... ♘cb4

Exploiting White's lack of development to grab the initiative.

11 ♕xd7+ ♗xd7 12 ♘xd5 exd5 13 a3 ♖c8+ 14 ♔b1 ♗f5+ 15 ♔a1 ♘c2+ 16 ♔a2 0-0 17 e3

South finds a brilliant way to expose White's king.

17 ... ♘xa3! 18 bxa3 ♖c2+ 19 ♔b3 ♗f6 20 ♖xd5 ♖b2+ 21 ♔c4 ♖c8+ 22 ♖c5 b5+ 23 ♔d5 ♖d2+ 0-1

after 4 ... c5

after 10 ... ♘cb4

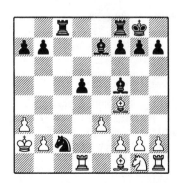

after 17 e3

Kings Indian: Classical 7 dxe5
Ryba-Hillarp Persson
Korinthos 1998

**1 d4 ♘f6 2 c4 g6 3 ♘f3 ♗g7 4
♘c3 0-0 5 e4 d6 6 ♗e2 e5 7 dxe5
dxe5 8 ♕xd8 ♖xd8**

This line is not as innocuous as it
looks although it is often played by
White in the mistaken belief that
Black must reconcile himself to an
instant draw.

9 ♗g5 ♘bd7

There are a variety of replies but
this is one of the best ways to head
for a middlegame battle.

10 ♖d1

White challenges for control of
the d-file with the bonus of threatening 11 ♘xe5. Others:

a) 10 0-0-0 ♖f8 11 ♘d5 c6 12
♘e7+ ♔h8 13 ♗e3 ♖e8 14 ♘xc8
♖axc8 15 ♘g5 ♖e7 Teixeira-
Zapata, Sao Paulo 1997.

b) 10 ♘d5 c6 11 ♘xf6+ ♘xf6 12
♘d2 (12 ♘xe5 ♖e8!=+) 12 ... h6 13
♗e3 ♘g4 14 ♗xg4 ♗xg4 15 f3
♗e6 16 ♔e2 f5= Gurevich-Sherzer,
Chicago 1992.

**10 ... ♖f8 11 0-0 c6 12 b4 ♖e8 13
c5 a5 14 a3 axb4 15 axb4 ♖a3**

Tiger (yes, that really is his name)
improves the posiitons of his pieces
and chips away at White's
solid-looking structure.

**16 ♖d3 ♖b3 17 ♘a2 ♖xd3 18
♗xd3 ♘f8 19 ♖b1 ♖d8 20 ♘xe5**

If 20 ♖d1 then 20 ... h6 21 ♗xf6
♗xf6 gives Black a pleasant ending
with the benefit of the two bishops.

**20 ... ♘e6 21 ♗xf6 ♗xf6 22
♘g4 ♗g7 23 ♘c1?**

Whoops!

23 ... ♘f4 0-1

after 8 ... ♖xd8

after 15 ... ♖a3

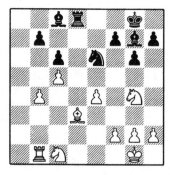

after 23 ♘c1

King's Indian: Samisch 6 ... c5
Gil-Howell
Gausdal 1986

1 d4 ♘f6 2 c4 g6 3 ♘c3 ♗g7 4 e4 d6 5 f3 0-0 6 ♗e3 c5 7 dxc5 dxc5 8 ♕xd8

The alternative 8 ♗xc5 gives Black compensation in the form of active pieces: 8 ... ♘c6 9 ♗e3 ♘d7 10 ♖c1 ♕a5 11 ♘h3 ♖d8 12 ♘f2 ♘c5 13 ♗d2 ♗xc3 14 bxc3 ♗e6 15 ♕c2 ♘e5=+ Dlugy-Gelfand, Palma de Mallorca 1989.

8 ... ♖xd8 9 ♗xc5

It used to be thought that Black must be seriously misguided to allow White to exchange queens and win a pawn. Nowadays, however, Black's lead in development and effective g7 bishop is considered more than sufficient compensation.

9 ... ♘c6 10 ♘d5 ♘d7!

A key move in reviving the whole line.

11 ♘xe7+ ♘xe7 12 ♗xe7 ♗xb2 13 ♖b1

Laco-Mohr, Portoroz 1996, continued 13 ♗xd8 ♗xa1 14 ♗c7 b6 15 g3 (White takes too long to develop) 15 ... ♗a6 16 ♗f4 ♘c5 17 ♔d2 ♖c8 18 ♘h3 ♘a4 19 ♘f2 ♗c3+ 20 ♔e3 ♖d8 21 ♘g4 h5 22 ♘h6+ ♔g7 23 ♔f2 ♗d2 and Black wins a piece.

13 ... ♗c3+ 14 ♔f2 ♗d4+ 15 ♔g3 ♖e8 16 ♗g5 ♘f6 17 ♘h3 ♘h5+ 18 ♔h4 ♔g7 19 g4

If 19 ♘f4 then 19 ... ♗f2+ 20 g3 ♘xf4 21 ♗xf4 f6 22 ♗c1 h5 and the white king is caught in a mating net.

19 ... h6 20 ♗xh6+ ♔xh6 21 gxh5 f5 22 ♔g3 fxe4 23 ♗g2 gxh5 24 f4 ♖g8+ 25 ♘g5 h4+ 0-1

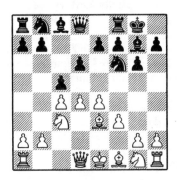

after 6 ... c5

after 9 ... ♘c6

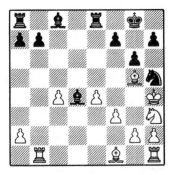

after 18 ♔h4

Pirc: 3 f3
Reilly-Leskiewicz
Melbourne 1998

1 d4 d6 2 e4 ♘f6 3 f3

Now 3 ... g6 4 c4 transposes to a Samisch King's Indian.

3 ... e5

Probably best.

4 dxe5

After 4 d5 ♗e7 5 ♗e3 0-0 6 ♕d2 ♘e8 7 ♗d3 h6 8 g3 ♗g5 9 h4 ♗xe3 10 ♕xe3 c6 11 c4 cxd5 12 cxd5 ♘d7 13 ♘c3 ♘c5 14 ♗c2 ♕b6 15 ♖b1 f5 Black had the initiative in Shetty-Komliakov, Calcutta 1998.

4 ... dxe5 5 ♕xd8+ ♔xd8 6 ♗c4

Black has given up the right to castle but in practice his king is very safe and the pawn on f3 makes it awkward for White to develop smoothly.

6 ... ♔e7

More usual and fine for Black are:

a) 6 ... ♔e8 7 ♗e3 ♘bd7 8 a4 a5 9 ♘a3 c6 10 ♘e2 ♗c5 11 ♔f2 ♗xe3+ 12 ♔xe3 ♘c5 13 b3 ♔e7 14 ♖hd1 ♘fd7 15 ♘c1 ♘b6 16 ♘d3 ♘xd3 17 ♖xd3 ♗d7 18 ♖ad1 ♖hd8 19 g3 ♗e8 20 f4 f6 21 ♖1d2 ½-½ Aagaard-Shaw, Rotherham 1997.

b) 6 ... ♗e6 7 ♗xe6 fxe6 8 ♘h3 ♗d6 9 ♘d2 ♔e7 10 ♘c4 ♘c6 11 ♗d2 b5 12 ♘e3 a6 gave White a minimal advantage in Bezgodov-S.Kasparov, Minsk 1998. Apparently Black is no relation to Garry!

7 ♘c3 ♗e6 8 ♘d5+ ♗xd5 9 exd5 ♔d6

Tempting White to chase the king but 9 ... ♘bd7 is best.

10 b3 ♘xd5 11 ♗a3+ ♔e6 12 ♗xd5+ ♔xd5 13 ♖d1+ ♔e6 14 ♖d8??

A nightmare

14 ... ♗b4+ 0-1

after 3 f3

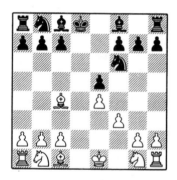

after 6 ♗c4

after 11 ... ♗b4+

Philidor: 4 ♕xd4
Luther-Maiwald
Gelsenkirchen 1998

1 e4 e5 2 ♘f3 d6 3 d4 exd4 4 ♕xd4

In place of the usual 4 ♘xd4.

4 ... a6

a) 4 ... ♗d7 and now:

a1) 5 ♗f4 ♘f6 6 ♘c3 ♘c6 7 ♕d2 ♗e7 8 h3 0-0 9 0-0-0 a6 10 e5 dxe5 11 ♘xe5 ♘xe5 12 ♗xe5+= Johansen-Kagan, Melbourne 1998.

a2) 5 ♗g5 ♕c8 6 ♘c3 ♘c6 7 ♕d2 h6 8 ♗e3 ♘f6 9 0-0-0 ♗e7 10 ♗c4 ♗e6 11 ♗b3 ♗xb3 12 axb3+= Gurevich-Remlinger, New York 1994.

b) 4 ... ♘e7 5 ♗g5 ♘bc6 6 ♕c3 (6 ♕d2!?) 6 ... f6 7 ♗h4 ♘g6 8 ♘bd2 ♘xh4 9 ♘xh4 ♕e7 10 0-0-0 g6 11 f4 ♗d7+= Kashtanov-Ivanov, St Petersburg 1998.

5 ♗f4 ♘c6 6 ♕d2 ♘f6 7 ♘c3 g6 8 0-0-0 ♗g7 9 e5 dxe5 10 ♕xd8+ ♘xd8 11 ♗xe5

Luther has a definite edge thanks to his pressure on c7 and space advantage.

11 ... ♘e6 12 ♗c4 0-0 13 ♖he1

It is tempting to go a pawn up with 13 ♗xe6 ♗xe6 14 ♗xc7 but this advantage disappears after 14 ... ♘g4 15 ♗g3 ♗xc3 16 bxc3 ♗xa2=.

13 ... b5 14 ♘d5 bxc4 15 ♘xf6+ ♗xf6 16 ♗xf6 ♗b7 17 ♘e5 ♗xg2 18 ♘d7 ♖fc8 19 ♗c3 h5?

19 ... ♖d8 is the only move but White is still slightly better after 20 ♗f6 ♖e8 21 ♗e5.

20 ♘f6+ ♔f8 21 ♖xe6!

Luther spots a mate.

21 ... fxe6 22 ♖d7 e5

What else? 22 ... ♗c6 23 ♗b4 mate.

23 ♗d2 1-0

after 4 ♕xd4

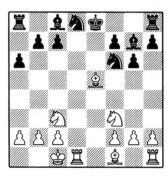

after 11 ♗xe5

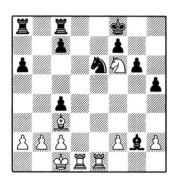

after 20 ... h5

Conclusion

The selection of games shows how often the course of a potentially long-drawn-out ending is abruptly changed by the introduction of a surprising tactic or rapid attack.

Positively-minded protagonists know that making things difficult for your opponent is the first step to success. In the game, Gil-Howell, Black relies on rapid piece development to commence a king hunt and this in turn provokes weaknesses which are then exploited.

In Reilly-Leskiewicz the main lesson to be learned is that one should remain ever vigilant.

The Art of Attack

1 Be on the look-out for all sorts of tactical tricks in the ending—this is not just a slow strategic phase of the game.

2 Bear in mind that an active king, as recommended by endgame principles, can also fall foul of a direct attack.

3 Some simplifying opening variations, such as the Spanish Exchange, are ideal for creating tactical situations based on clearly-defined plans already adopted in master games.

The Art of Defence

1 Remember that tactics do not stop just because queens have been exchanged. Obvious perhaps, but, judging by the examples, something which is easily forgotten.

2 Castle early and try to avoid a passive position.

3 If in doubt, counter-attack.

8 Opening Surprises

A man surprised is half beaten. The moment you surprise your opponent is often the moment you can begin to dictate the course of the game.

Many players concentrate on just getting their pieces out with dull, routine play. One can sympathise with them because few people have the time to study the latest twist on, say, move 19 of a certain line, especially when more often than not the game will have deviated well before then. However, the extremely early opening surprises presented in this chapter have a much better chance of appearing on your board. Here your preparation will *not* be wasted, and your opponents, having to rely on their own resources, will have a hard time knowing what to do next. Most popular openings are represented here—with interesting possibilities for both White and Black.

In the game, Korchnoi-Sutovsky, White amazes as early as move five. Looking just like a typical beginner's mistake, this crazy knight move this should mislead your opponent into thinking that your opening repertoire is suspect. However, the analysis supporting the idea is sound and will prove to be a big asset to you.

The idea of moving your knight to the edge of the board to provoke the opponent is also explored in Cladouras-Stein and Froehlich-Miles, where each time the innovator triumphs.

It is always satisfying to revive successfully old lines which have been unfairly dismissed. Loginov-Sakaev shows Black cultivating an old idea of Spassky's and creating a strong attack.

The Budapest Gambit has the advantage of being played as early as the second move so Demirel-Kogan and Abatino-Chatalbashev should provide you with enough live ammunition to come out with all guns blazing.

And if you want something completely different why not try the Elephant Gambit? The fine game, Dodson-Rogers, shows just what Black is capable of.

Remember—who dares, wins!

Grunfeld 5 ♘a4
Korchnoi-Sutovsky
Dresden Zonal 1998

1 d4 ♘f6 2 c4 g6 3 ♘c3 d5 4 cxd5 ♘xd5 5 ♘a4

An absolutely sensational move! The fact it has been endorsed at the highest level by a player of Korchnoi's stature means that it has to be taken seriously. The reason for all the fuss is because this move of the knight to the edge of the board is not considered worthy of mention by any of the opening books. It was the Armenian player Nadanian who tested and developed the ideas behind the system. The basic reasoning is that in the main line 5 e4 ♘xc3 6 bxc3 Black will continue with ... ♗g7 and ... c5, undermining the centre pawns, whereas after the text White no longer has to worry about this potential weakness on c3 and it is more difficult to play ... c5. If Black now makes a routine response, White can continue with e4 and simply develop his pieces.

5 ... ♗g7

If 5 ... e5 then 6 dxe5 ♗b4+ 7 ♗d2 ♘e3 8 fxe3 ♗xd2+ 9 ♕xd2 ♕h4+ 10 g3 ♕xa4 11 ♕d4 is in White's favour because the tripled pawns control several important squares.

6 e4 ♘b6

In the game, Toulzac-Varlet, Montpellier 1998, Black tried 6 ... ♘b4. The game continued: 7 a3 (7 ♘f3? ♗xd4! 8 ♘xd4 ♕xd4 9 ♕xd4 ♘c2+ wins) 7 ... ♘4a6?! (7 ... ♘c6 8 d5 looks a better bet for Black) 8 ♗e3 0-0 9 ♗e2 e5 10 ♘f3 exd4 11 ♗xd4 ♗xd4 12 ♕xd4 ♕xd4 13 ♘xd4 ♖d8 14 0-0-0 c6 15 ♘f5!

after 5 ♘a4

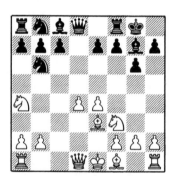

after 8 ♘f3

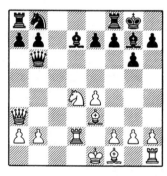

after 13 ... ♘xd4

♖d7 16 ♘e7+ ♖xe7 17 ♖d8+ ♔g7
18 ♖xc8 ±.

7 ♗e3 0-0

a) 7 ... e5 8 d5 0-0 9 ♘f3 c6 10
♘xb6 axb6 11 ♗c4 b5 12 ♗b3 ♘a6
13 0-0 ♘c7 14 dxc6 ♕xd1 15
♖fxd1 bxc6 16 ♖ac1 ♗e6 17 ♖xc6
Rowson-Knott, British National
League (4NCL) 1998.

b) 7 ... ♘c6 8 ♗b5 ♗d7 9 ♘c5!
♕c8 10 ♖c1 ♘b8 11 ♗e2 0-0 12 h4
1-0 Paramos-Herrero, Mondariz
1997.

8 ♘f3

White is developing normally but
there are still obstacles for Black to
overcome.

8 ... ♘xa4

The game Yegiazarian-Neverov,
Minsk 1998, continued 8 ... ♗g4 9
♗e2 ♘c6 10 d5! ♗xf3 11 gxf3 ♘e5
12 ♖c1 ♘ed7 13 ♘c3 c6 14 dxc6
bxc6 and now instead of 15 f4?! as
played which can be well met by 15
... e5 White should try 15 h4! e5 16
♘a4 ♖c8 17 ♘c5 ♕e7 18 a4+=
according to Nadanian and
Yegiazarian.

**9 ♕xa4 c5 10 ♖d1 ♕b6 11 ♖d2
♗d7 12 ♕a3 cxd4 13 ♘xd4 ♕c7
14 ♗e2 e5 15 ♖c2**

Korchnoi later suggested 15 ♘b5!
when White is better after 15 ...
♗xb5 16 ♗xb5 a6 17 0-0 ♘c6 18
♗c4.

**15 ... ♕d8 16 ♘b5 ♘c6 17 ♘d6
♕b8 18 ♗c4 ♘d4 19 ♗xd4 exd4
20 0-0 ♗e6?**

The last chance for Sutovsky is 20
... ♗e5 but Korchnoi is still the favourite after 21 ♘xf7 ♖xf7 22 f4
♗g7 23 ♕b3.

**21 ♗xe6 fxe6 22 ♖fc1 ♗e5 23
♖c7 ♗xd6 24 ♕xd6 ♖f7 25 ♕xe6
1-0**

after 15 ♖c2

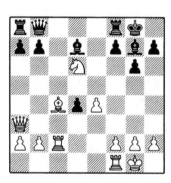

after 20 0-0

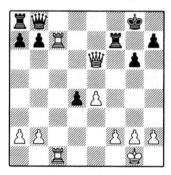

after 25 ♕xe6

Spanish: 5 ... ♘a5
Cladouras-Stein
Bundesliga 1990

1 e4 e5 2 ♘f3 ♘c6 3 ♗b5 a6 4 ♗a4 b5 5 ♗b3 ♘a5

This looks like an obvious opening mistake but it has been played by Fischer and Taimanov. The truth is that attempts by White at outright refutation are fruitless and a long-term positional strategy is needed.

6 0-0

The other moves:

a) 6 ♘xe5 ♘xb3 7 axb3 ♕g5 (7 ... ♕e7!?) 8 d4 ♕xg2 9 ♕f3 ♕xf3 10 ♘xf3 ♗b7 11 0-0 f5 12 ♖e1 fxe4 13 ♘g5 d5 14 ♗f4 ♗d6=+ Neumann-Stein, Bundesliga 1984.

b) 6 ♗xf7+?! ♔xf7 7 ♘xe5+ ♔e7! 8 d4 ♘f6 9 ♕f3 ♗b7 10 b4 ♘c4 11 ♕e2 ♘xe5 12 dxe5 ♘xe4 13 f3 ♔e8 14 0-0 (14 fxe4 ♕h4+ wins) 14 ..♘g5 15 f4 ♘e4 and the White attack has fizzled out, Rabar-Taimanov, Belgrade 1956.

6 ... d6 7 d4 ♘xb3

Black achieves a straightforward exchange of the bishop which is so often White's trump card in the Spanish. The price is a lack of development but this is, however, difficult to exploit.

8 axb3 exd4 9 ♘xd4 ♗b7 10 ♖e1 g6 11 ♘c3 ♗g7 12 ♗f4

Another idea is 11 ♕d3 followed by ♗g5.

12 ... ♘f6 13 ♕d2 0-0 14 ♗g5 ♕d7 15 ♗xf6 ♗xf6 16 ♘d5 ♗g7 17 c4 ♖ad8 18 cxb5 axb5 19 ♖a7 c5 20 ♘f5?

An error but 20 ♘f3 b4 is slightly better for Black.

20 ... gxf5 21 exf5 ♖fe8 22 f6 ♕c6 23 ♖xb7 ♕xd5! 0-1

after 5 ... ♘a5

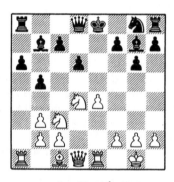

after 11 ... ♗g7

after 23 ♖xb7

Sicilian: 3 ... ♘a5
Froehlich-Miles
Bad Wörishofen 1997

1 e4 c5 2 ♘f3 ♘c6 3 ♗b5 ♘a5

A startling move for White to cope with when his main plan is to exchange on c6! It has been known for some time but Miles has catapulted it into the limelight.

4 0-0

Also possible:

a) 4 ♗e2 b6 5 ♘c3 ♗b7 6 d4 cxd4 7 ♘xd4 g6 8 ♗e3 ♗g7 9 0-0 ♘f6 10 e5 ♘e4 11 ♘xe4 ♗xe4= Jakupovic-Kozul, Sarajevo 1998.

b) 4 d4 a6 5 ♗e2 cxd4 6 ♘xd4 b5 7 0-0 ♗b7 8 ♕d3+= Prokopchuk-Chernyshov, Pardubice 1997.

c) 4 c3 a6 5 ♗a4 b5 6 ♗c2 d5 (6 ... d6!?) 7 0-0 ♗b7 8 exd5 ♗xd5 9 d4 ♘b7 10 ♗e3 e6 11 ♘bd2 ♘f6 12 ♘e5 ♗e7= Kierzek-Simic, Bled 1996

4 ... a6 5 ♗e2 e6 6 d4 cxd4 7 c3?!

White wants to develop quickly but it is not worth a pawn. 7 ♘xd4 is better 7 ... ♕c7 8 b3 ♘f6 9 ♗f3 d6 10 c4+=.

7 ... dxc3 8 ♘xc3 b5 9 ♗f4 ♗b7 10 ♖c1 ♖c8 11 ♕d2 ♘e7 12 ♖fd1 ♘g6 13 ♗g3 ♗e7 14 h4?!

Froehlich is trying to prove some compensation for the pawn but this just weakens his own set-up. 14 ♗d6 is an option but Miles is still the favourite to win.

14 ... h5 15 ♘e5 ♘xe5 16 ♗xe5 0-0 17 ♗xh5 ♗xh4 18 ♕xd7 ♗xf2+!

Miles wrecks White's kingside and picks up a pawn in the process.

19 ♔xf2 ♕h4+ 20 ♔g1 ♕xh5 21 ♗c7 0-1

after 3 ... ♘a5

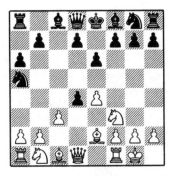

after 7 c3

after 18 ♕xd7

Reti: 2 ... b5
Loginov-Sakaev
St.Petersburg Championship 1996

1 ♘f3 ♘f6 2 g3 b5
This variation is named after
Boris Spassky who employed it
against Petrosian in the 1966 World
Championship match. In queenside
openings White usually includes a
pawn advance to c4 in his plans. But
now this pawn can simply be taken.
Moreover, the power of White's
bishop on g2 is ready to be chal-
lenged by a counter-fianchetto on
b7.
3 ♘a3

a) 3 c3 c5 4 ♗g2 ♗b7 5 0-0 e6 6
d3 ♗e7 7 a4 b4 8 ♘bd2 a5 9 e4 d5=
Walker-Knox, British Champ. 1994.

b) 3 a4 b4 4 ♗g2 ♗b7 5 0-0 e6 6
d3 d5 7 ♘bd2 ♘bd7 8 e4 dxe4 9
♘g5 ♗e7 10 ♘gxe4 ♗d5=
Summerscale-Arkell, 1994.

c) 3 ♗g2 ♗b7 4 0-0 e6 5 d3 d5 6
♘bd2 c5 7 e4 ♗e7 8 ♖e1 ♘c6 9 c3
0-0 10 e5 ♘e8 11 d4 b4= Petrovic-
Timoshenko, Nova Gorica 1997.
3 ... a6 4 c4 e5!?
A surprise because only 4 ... b4 or
4 ... e6 are normally considered.
5 ♕b3

a) 5 cxb5 e4 6 ♘d4 ♗c5 7 ♘ac2
♘g4 (7 ... ♗b7!?) 8 h3 ♘xf2 9
♔xf2 ♕f6+ 10 ♔e3 ♕g5+ 11 ♔f2=

b) 5 ♘xe5 ♗b7 6 ♘f3 ♗xa3 7
bxa3 ♗xf3 8 exf3 0-0 gives Black
enough compensation for the
material.
**5 ... e4 6 ♘h4 ♗c5 7 ♘c2 d5 8
d4? exd3 9 ♕xd3 ♘c6 10 cxd5**

10 cxb5 is well met by 10 ... ♘e5
11 ♕d1 ♘eg4 12 e3 ♘e4-+.
**10 ... ♘e5 11 ♕c3 ♗xf2+! 12
♔d1 ♕xd5+ 13 ♗d2 ♘e4 0-1**

after 2 ... b5

after 4 ... e5

after 11 ♕c3

French: 2 ♕e2
Wohl-Garcia Santos
Malaga 1998

1 e4 e6 2 ♕e2

The early queen move leads to unusual positions. Chigorin's original intention was to meet 2 ... d5 with 3 exd5 ♕xd5 4 ♘c3+=.

2 ... e5

Black attempts to show the queen is awkwardly placed. Or:

a) 2 ... ♗e7 3 g3 d5 4 d3 dxe4 5 dxe4 b6 6 ♘f3 ♗a6 7 c4 ♘c6 8 ♘c3 ♗b4 9 ♗d2 e5 10 0-0-0 ♘d4 11 ♘xd4 exd4 12 ♘d5+= Vasiukov-Volkov, Moscow 1995.

b) 2 ... c5 3 f4 ♘c6 4 ♘f3 ♗e7 5 d3 d6 (5 ... d5 is the best move giving Black equal chances) 6 ♗e3 ♘f6 7 ♘bd2 ♕a5 8 c3 b5 9 h3 b4 10 c4 b3 11 a3 and the weak pawn on b3 became a liability in Sarthou-Goldgewicht, Montpellier 1998.

c) 2 ... ♘f6 3 e5 ♘d5 4 ♘f3 d6 5 d4 ♘e7 6 h4 b6 7 ♘c3 d5 8 ♕d1 ♗a6 9 ♗xa6 ♘xa6 10 ♘e2 ♕d7 11 c3+= Ehlvest-Vaganian, Novgorod 1995.

3 ♘f3 ♘c6 4 ♕b5

Incredibly, the Australian international has decided to play a Spanish with his queen fulfilling the role of the bishop. In Rodriguez-Bronstein, Clarin 1997, White sensibly tried 4 g3 to develop the bishop without having to move the queen. Then followed 4 g3 g6 5 ♗g2 ♗g7 6 c3 ♘f6 7 d4 d6 8 0-0 0-0 9 dxe5 ♘xe5 10 ♘xe5 dxe5 11 ♘d2=.

4 ... d6 5 ♗c4 ♗d7 6 ♕b3 ♕f6 7 0-0 ♘a5 8 ♕c3 ♘xc4 9 ♕xc4 0-0-0 10 ♘c3 ♕e6 11 ♘d5 ♗c6 12 d3 h6 13 ♕b3 f5??

13 ... ♘f6 is better.

14 ♘b6+ 1-0

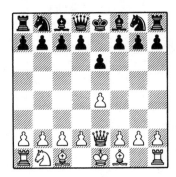

after 2 ♕e2

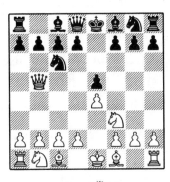

after 4 ♕b5

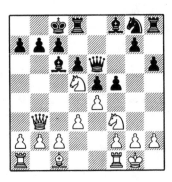

after 13 ... f5

Budapest: Fajarowicz 4 ♘d2
Demirel-Kogan
Vlissingen 1996

1 d4 ♘f6 2 c4 e5 3 dxe5 ♘e4

This variation has been popular ever since Fajarowicz played it against Steiner at Wiesbaden in 1928!

4 ♘d2

a) 4 a3 b6 5 ♘d2 (5 ♕d5 ♘c5! 6 ♕xa8 ♗b7 7 ♕xa7 ♘c6 when the queens leaves the board) 5 ... ♗b7 6 ♘xe4 ♗xe4 7 ♗f4 ♕e7 8 e3 ♗b7 9 ♕c2 g6 10 ♘f3 ♗g7 11 ♗e2 ♘c6 12 ♗g5 ♕e6 13 0-0-0 0-0 and Black will restore material equality, Miralles-Toulzac, Mulhouse 1998.

b) 4 ♕c2 d5 5 ♘f3 (5 exd6!? should be considered) 5 ... ♗f5 6 ♕b3 ♘c5 7 ♕d1 ♘c6 8 a3 dxc4 9 ♕xd8+ ♖xd8 10 ♗g5 ♗e7 11 ♗xe7 ♔xe7 12 ♘bd2 b5 13 ♘h4 ♗e6 14 g3 ♖xd2 0-1 Linn-Braemigk, Trier 1992.

4 ... ♘c5 5 ♘gf3 ♘c6 6 b3 g5

A stunning way to create double-edged play. A bishop on g7 and the menace of g5-g4 combine to thwart White's efforts to hold on to the e5 pawn.

7 ♗b2 ♗g7 8 e3 d6 9 ♗e2 dxe5

Kogan has a comfortable position and White is unable to open up the position in an effort to exploit the pawn on g5.

10 0-0 ♗f5 11 b4 ♘xb4 12 ♗xe5 ♗xe5 13 ♘xe5 ♕d6 14 e4 ♕xe5 15 exf5 0-0-0

The pin on the d-file is ominous for White and he also has to cope with ... ♘bd3 when Black dominates the game.

16 ♗f3 ♕c3 17 ♘e4 ♘xe4 18 ♕a4 ♘d2 19 ♕xa7 ♘xf3+ 20 gxf3 ♘c6 21 ♖ab1 0-1

after 3 ... ♘e4

after 6 ... g5

after 15 ... 0-0-0

Budapest: 4 ♗f4
Abatino-Chatalbashev
Cutro 1998

1 d4 ♘f6 2 c4 e5 3 dxe5 ♘g4

The Budapest Gambit relies on rapid piece development as compensation for the pawn deficit.

4 ♗f4

a) 4 e3 ♘xe5 5 ♘h3 and now:

a1) 5 ... ♗b4+ 6 ♗d2 a5 7 ♘f4 ♘a6 8 ♗e2 ♘c5 9 0-0 ♖a6 10 ♗c3 ♗xc3 11 ♘xc3 ♖h6 12 g3 d6 13 a3 g5 14 ♘h5 ♕d7 15 f4 gxf4 16 exf4 ♘c6 17 b4 ♘e6 18 ♘d5± Lima-De Andrade, Brasilia 1998.

a2) 5 ... g6 6 ♘f4 ♗g7 7 ♘c3 0-0 8 ♗e2 d6 9 0-0 a5 10 ♕c2 ♘a6 11 ♖d1 ♘c5 12 f3 b6 13 ♗d2 ♗d7 14 ♗e1 ♖c8 15 ♗f2 f5 16 ♘d3 ♘cxd3 ½-½ Mah-Pert, Witley 1998.

b) 4 e4 ♘xe5 5 f4 ♘g6 (5 ... ♘ec6 is also good) 6 ♗e3 ♗b4+ 7 ♘d2 ♕e7 8 ♗d3 ♕d6 9 ♗c2 ♘xf4 10 ♕g4 ♘g6 11 0-0-0 ♘c6 12 ♘gf3 ♕e7 with an extra pawn for Black, Lorscheid-Dunnington, Ostend 1992.

c) 4 ♘f3 ♗c5 5 e3 ♘c6 6 ♘c3 0-0 7 ♗e2 ♖e8 8 0-0 ♘cxe5 9 ♘xe5 ♘xe5 10 b3 a5 11 ♗b2 ♖a6 12 ♘a4 ♗f8 13 f4 ♘c6 14 c5 ♖a8 15 ♖f3 d6 16 cxd6 ♕xd6 17 ♕xd6 ♗xd6 18 ♖g3 ♗f8 19 ♘c3 ½-½ Shaked-Lalic, London 1997.

d) 4 ♕d4 d6 5 exd6 ♗xd6 6 ♕e4+?! (6 ♘f3!?) 6 ... ♗e6 7 ♘c3 0-0 8 ♘f3 ♕d7 9 ♘d4 ♗xc4 10 ♘f5 ♗e6 11 ♘xd6 cxd6 12 g3 d5 13 ♕f4 d4 14 ♘e4 ♗d5 15 f3 f5 16 ♘c5 ♕e7 17 ♘d3 ♘c6 18 h3 ♘ge5 19 ♘xe5 ♘xe5 20 ♔f2 d3 21 ♗d2 dxe2 22 ♗xe2 ♗xf3 23 ♗b4 ♕e6 24 ♖he1 ♗xe2 25 ♕e3 f4 0-1 Beliavsky-Epishin, Reggio Emilia, 1991.

after 3 ... ♘g4

after 5 ... d6

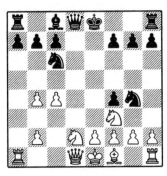

after 8 ... ♘c6

4 ... ♗b4+ 5 ♘d2 d6

A relatively new idea to maintain the initiative. 5 ♘f3 ♘c6 is more common.

6 a3

Alternatively:

a) 6 ♘gf3 dxe5 7 ♘xe5 ♗xd2+ 8 ♕xd2 ♕xd2+ 9 ♔xd2 ♘xf2 10 ♖g1 ♘a6 11 ♘d3 ♘e4+ 12 ♔e3 ♘f6 13 h3 ♗d7 14 ♗e5 0-0-0 ½-½ Gomez Esteban-Mohr, Maribor 1995.

b) 6 exd6 ♕f6 7 ♘h3 ♘xf2 8 ♔xf2 ♗xh3 9 g3 ♗xf1 10 ♖xf1 ♕d4+ 11 ♔g2 ♗xd6 12 ♕b3 ♘d7 (12 ... 0-0!?) 13 ♗e3 ♕e5 14 c5± Summerscale-Szabolcsi, French Team Championship 1996.

6 ... dxe5 7 axb4 exf4 8 ♘gf3 ♘c6 9 g3 fxg3 10 hxg3 ♘xb4 11 ♕a4+ ♘c6 12 ♕c2

White has emerged from the opening minus a pawn and desperately needing to catch up in development.

12 ... h6 13 ♗g2 0-0 14 0-0 ♖e8 15 e3 ♕f6 16 ♖ac1 ♗f5

Black has a clear advantage.

17 ♕b3 ♖ab8 18 ♕a3 a5 19 ♕c5 ♖bd8 20 ♖fe1 b6 21 ♕b5 ♘b4 22 ♖c3 ♘d3 23 ♖f1 ♘c5 0-1

White can do little against the threat of 24 ... ♗d7 which traps the queen. For instance: 24 ♘d4 ♗d7 25 ♗c6 ♗xc6 26 ♘xc6 ♖xd2-+.

after 12 ♕c2

after 16 ... ♗f5

after 23 ... ♘c5

Caro-Kann: 3 ♕f3
Kennaugh-Houska
British Championship 1998

1 e4 c6 2 ♘c3 d5 3 ♕f3
A good way to avoid the main lines while at the same time giving Black a few early problems.
3 ... e6
The solid reply. Other moves are:
a) 3 ... d4 4 ♗c4! ♘f6 (4 ... dxc3 5 ♕xf7+ ♔d7 6 dxc3 gives a strong attack) 5 e5 dxc3 6 exf6 cxd2+ 7 ♗xd2 exf6 8 0-0-0 ♗e7 9 ♕g3+=.
b) 3 ... dxe4 4 ♘xe4 ♘d7 5 d4 ♘df6 6 c3 ♘xe4 7 ♕xe4 ♘f6 8 ♕c2 ♕d5 9 ♘f3 ♗f5 10 ♕b3 ♕xb3 11 axb3 a6 12 b4= Totsky-Shovunov, Maikop 1998.
c) 3 ... ♘f6 4 e5 ♘fd7 5 d4 e6 6 ♘h3 a6 7 ♘g5 ♕e7 8 ♗d3 c5 9 ♘e2 cxd4 10 ♕g3 f6 11 ♘f3 ♘xe5 12 ♘xe5 fxe5 13 ♗xh7 ♘c6 14 0-0 ♔d7 15 ♗g6 ♕f6 16 f4 e4 17 f5 ♗d6 18 ♗f4 ♗e5 19 fxe6+ ♕xe6 20 ♗f7!± Galego-Izeta, Seville 1992.
4 d4 ♘f6 5 ♗g5 dxe4
Arapovic-Campora, Mendrisio 1988, continued instead 5 ... ♗e7 6 e5 ♘fd7 7 ♗xe7 ♕xe7 8 ♕g3 0-0 9 f4 c5 10 ♘f3 cxd4 11 ♘xd4 ♘c6 12 0-0-0 f6 13 ♘xd5! ♕f7 (13 ... exd5 14 ♘f5 ♕f7 15 ♘h6+ wins) 14 ♘c7 with a big advantage.
6 ♘xe4 ♘bd7 7 0-0-0 ♗e7 8 ♗c4 0-0 9 ♘e2
The position has similarities to a French Defence but with the pawn on c6 Black's pieces are too passive.
9 ... ♘xe4 10 ♗xe7 ♕xe7 11 ♕xe4 ♘f6 12 ♕h4 b5 13 ♗d3 c5??
A blunder, but 13 ... h6 14 ♖he1 is still slightly better for White.
14 ♗xh7+ 1-0

after 3 ♕f3

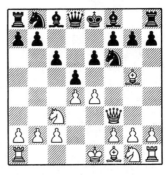

after 5 ♗g5

after 13 ... c5

Trompowsky: 2 ... ♘e4
Bellon Lopez-Del Campo
Cuba 1998

1 d4 ♘f6 2 ♗g5 ♘e4 3 ♗h4
Though 3 ♗f4 is now established
as the main move, the text also has a
lot of merit.
3 ... c5 4 f3 g5 5 fxe4 gxh4 6 e3
White has a wretched pawn structure but the open lines provide
plenty of attacking opportunities.
6 ... ♕b6
The critical move has to be 6 ...
♗h6 when White has tried the
amazing 7 ♔f2 and lived to tell the
tale. A challenging idea is 7 ♗c4 to
exert pressure on f7. Zlochevsky-
Horvath, Bozen 1998, continued 7
... ♕b6 (7 ... ♗xe3 8 ♕f3) 8 ♘c3
♘c6 9 ♘ge2 ♗xe3 10 ♘d5 ♕a5+
11 b4 ♘xb4 12 ♘xe3 cxd4 13 0-0
dxe3 14 ♗xf7+ ♔d8 15 ♕d4 ♖f8
16 ♕g7+-.
7 ♘c3! ♗g7
The tempting 7 ... ♕xb2 leaves
Black's king stranded after 8 ♘d5
♔d8 9 ♖b1 ♕a3 10 ♕h5 ♕xa2 11
♖d1 ♘c6 12 ♘f3 ♕a5+ 13 ♔f2
cxd4 14 exd4 e6 15 ♕g5+ ♘e7 16
♘e5 exd5 17 ♘xf7+ ♔e8 18 ♘xh8
♕b6 19 ♗e2 dxe4 20 ♗h5+ ♔d8 21
♖he1 1-0 Gorelov-Kuzmin, Moscow Champioinship 1988.
8 ♘d5 ♕d6 9 ♕g4 ♔f8 10 ♘f3
White is up against strong opposi-
tion but he has managed to create an
overwhelming position directly
from the opening.
**10 ... e6 11 ♕xh4 ♘c6 12 e5 ♕b8
13 ♘f6 d6 14 ♗b5 dxe5 15 ♗xc6
bxc6 16 ♘xe5 ♕b4+ 17 c3 ♕xb2
18 0-0**
White's assault nears a crescendo.
**18 ... ♕xc3 19 ♘d5 ♗f6 20 ♕xf6
1-0**

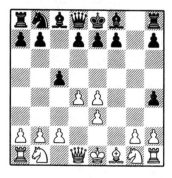

after 6 e3

after 10 ♘f3

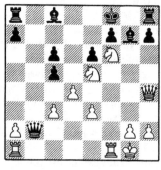

after 18 0-0

Sicilian: Kan 6 ♘d2
Carlsson-Mortensen
Copenhagen 1998

1 e4 c5 2 ♘f3 e6 3 d4 cxd4 4 ♘xd4 a6 5 ♗d3 ♘f6

The most popular square for the knight. In Lesiege-Hellsten, Bermuda 1997, Black experimented with 5 ... ♘e7 and there followed 6 0-0 ♘bc6 7 ♗e3 ♘xd4 8 ♗xd4 ♘c6 9 ♗e3 ♗e7 10 ♘d2 ♖b8 11 f4 d5 12 exd5 exd5 13 f5 0-0 14 ♕h5 ♖e8 15 ♖f3 ♗f8 16 ♖h3 h6 17 ♗xh6!+-.

6 ♘d2

The text is rarely seen. The main moves are 6 c4 or 6 0-0.

6 ... d5

The highly-rated Danish player takes the opportunity to challenge the centre, but this advance is flawed. In the game Shikhman-Hernandez, Chicago 1993, Black kept an eye on the e4-e5 advance by 6 ... ♕c7. The game continued 7 ♕e2 d6 8 0-0 ♗e7 9 ♔h1 ♘bd7 10 c4 0-0 11 f4 b6 12 ♘4b3 ♗b7 13 ♘f3 e5 14 f5 ♘c5 15 ♘xc5 dxc5 16 ♖g1 ♖ad8 17 ♗c2 ♖fe8 18 ♗d2 ♗f8 19 g4+=.

7 e5 ♘fd7

7 ... ♕b6 is necessary.

8 ♘xe6!

A gaping hole is created in the heart of Black's camp.

8 ... fxe6 9 ♕h5+ g6 10 ♗xg6+ hxg6 11 ♕xg6+ ♔e7 12 ♘c4!

This brilliant idea, exploiting the vulnerability of Black's king, had to be seen in advance.

12 ... ♗h6 13 ♗g5+ ♔f8

A grim retreat but the alternative is 13 ... ♗xg5 14 ♕g7+ ♔e8 15 ♘d6 mate.

14 ♗xd8 dxc4 15 ♗c7 ♗g7 16 ♕xe6 1-0

after 6 ♘d2

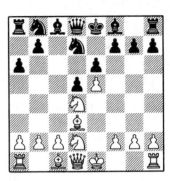

after 7 ♘fd7

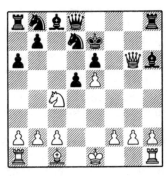

after 12 ... ♗h6

Spanish: Berlin 4 d4
Zapata-Antoniou
Elista Olympiad 1998

1 e4 e5 2 ♘f3 ♘c6 3 ♗b5 ♘f6
The solid Berlin variation.
4 d4!?
Steering the game towards a critical position at the earliest opportunity; the usual line is 4 0-0 ♘xe4 5 d4 ♘d6 6 ♗xc6 dxc6 7 dxe5 ♘f5 8 ♕xd8+ with the slightly better ending for White.
4 ... exd4

a) 4 ... ♘xd4 5 ♘xd4 c6 6 ♗c4 exd4 7 ♕xd4 ♕b6 8 ♕d3 ♗b4+ 9 c3 ♗c5 10 0-0 d5 11 exd5 0-0 12 b4 cxd5 13 ♗xd5 ♘xd5 14 ♕xd5 ♗e7 15 ♗e3 left White with an extra pawn in Kaminski-Keitlinghaus, Lazne Bohdanec 1996.

b) 4 ... ♘xe4 5 ♕e2 ♘d6 6 ♗xc6 dxc6 7 dxe5 ♘f5 8 ♗g5 ♗e7 9 ♗xe7 ♕xe7 10 ♘c3 ♗e6 11 0-0-0+= Zapata-Mitkov, Erevan Olympiad 1996

5 0-0 ♗c5
5 ... ♗e7 is better when White continues 6 ♖e1, intending e4-e5, before taking on d4.
6 e5 ♘d5 7 c3 0-0 8 cxd4 ♗e7 9 ♕b3 ♘b6 10 d5
The central pawns have become a dominant force, obliging the knight to return to its original square.
10 ... ♘b8 11 d6 cxd6 12 exd6 ♗xd6 13 a4 a5 14 ♗d3 ♘c6 15 ♗xh7+!
Congratulations! The Greek Gift is always a dangerous weapon.
15 ... ♔xh7 16 ♘g5+ ♔g6 17 ♕d3+ f5 18 ♕xd6+ ♕f6 19 ♕g3 f4 20 ♗xf4 1-0
Black resigned in view of 20 ... ♕xf4 21 ♘e6+! ♕xg3 22 ♘xf8+ ♔h6 23 fxg3+-.

after 4 d4

after 10 d5

after 14 ... ♘c6

Spanish: Delayed Exchange
McDonald-Wells
London 1998

1 e4 e5 2 ♘f3 ♘c6 3 ♗b5 a6 4 ♗a4 ♘f6 5 0-0 ♗e7 6 ♗xc6

This delayed capture on c6 aims to exploit the kingside pawn majority traditionally associated with the Spanish Exchange Variation - but without the need to swap queens.

6 ... dxc6 7 ♕e2 ♗g4 8 h3 ♗h5 9 g4

McDonald follows an old Russian recommendation to win a pawn, assessed as leading to an 'unclear' position. A quieter continuation, 9 d3, was selected in the game Ristic-Michalczak, Bundesliga 1995, and the battle got under way in the middlegame: 9 d3 ♗d6 10 ♘bd2 ♘d7 11 ♘c4 f6 12 ♘e3 ♘c5 13 ♘f5 ♘e6 14 c3 c5 15 a3 ♕d7 16 b4 0-0-0 17 ♗e3+=.

9 ... ♗g6 10 ♘xe5 ♗xe4 11 g5 ♖g8!

A star move. At a stroke Wells finds a way to refute White's set-up and so relegate the line in future opening books to a minor footnote.

12 d3

If 12 gxf6 Black wins after 12 ... gxf6+ 13 ♘g4 f5 14 f3 ♗d5 15 d3 h5 or 12 ♘g4 is rebuffed by 12 ... ♗xc2! 13 gxf6 gxf6 intending ... ♗d3 and ... f5.

12 ... ♗f5 13 ♖e1 ♗xh3 14 ♔h2 ♗e6 15 gxf6 gxf6 16 ♘f3

16 ♘c4 merely delays the inevitable upon 16 ... ♕d5 17 ♖g1 0-0-0 18 ♗f4 ♕f5-+.

16 ... ♕d5 17 ♔h1 ♗d6 0-1

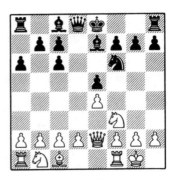

after 7 ♕e2

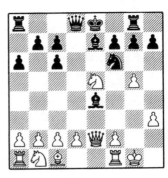

after 11 ... ♖g8

after 17 ... ♗d6

Blackmar-Diemer Gambit: 5 ... e6
Szenetra-Thiele
Deizisau 1998

1 d4 ♘f6 2 ♘c3 d5 3 e4 dxe4 4 f3

The Blackmar-Diemer Gambit is a romantic opening, sacrificing a pawn for a direct attack which often rewards White with a spectacular victory. Since the publication of my book on this opening I have found that a great deal of interest has been generated in the gambit. Inevitably, some lines have wobbled under closer scrutiny but practitioners have found plenty of new ideas for White.

4 ... exf3 5 ♘xf3 e6

The Euwe Defence has a sound reputation. Instead Lane-Dutton, Dartington 1995, continued 5 ... g6 6 ♗d3 (6 ♗c4 is the standard move) 6 ... ♗g7 7 0-0 0-0 8 ♕e1 (the illustrative game is a reminder that this is a standard theme) 8 ... ♘bd7 9 ♕h4 c5 10 d5 b6 11 ♗h6 ♗b7 12 ♘g5 ♕c7 13 ♘e4 ♕e5 14 ♗xg7 ♕e5 15 ♘xf6 ♘xf6 16 ♖xf6! ♕xd5 17 ♖xf7+! ♖xf7 18 ♕xh7+ ♔f6 19 ♕xg6+ ♔e5 20 ♘xf7+ ♔d4 21 ♕g4+ ♔e3 22 ♕e2+ ♔f4 23 g3 mate.

6 ♗d3 ♗e7 7 0-0 0-0 8 ♕e1

An easy transfer of the queen to the kingside to help in the attack.

8 ... c5 9 dxc5 ♗xc5+ 10 ♔h1 ♘c6 11 ♗g5 h6 12 ♕h4 ♗e7

12 ... hxg5 fails after 13 ♘xg5 ♖e8 14 ♖xf6 ♕xf6 15 ♖f1 ♕xf1+ 16 ♗xf1 ♗d4 17 ♕h5!±.

13 ♗xh6! ♘e8

If 13 ... gxh6 14 ♕xh6 and ♘g5 wins.

14 ♗g5 f5 15 ♖ad1 ♗d7 16 ♗c4 ♘f6 17 ♖fe1 ♕c8 18 ♖xd7 1-0

after 4 f3

after 8 ♕e1

after 12 ... ♗e7

Unorthodox Knight Hop
Mueller-Pieper
Eppingen 1988

1 e4 e5 2 ♘f3 ♘c6 3 ♗c4 ♘d4

Guaranteed to make a player with the White pieces smile. Though long considered a beginner's move it has been adopted as a surprise weapon even by internationals.

4 ♘xe5?

An attempt at outright refutation is a mistake. Also possible are:

a) 4 d3 ♘xf3+ 5 ♕xf3 ♕f6 6 ♕e2 ♗c5 7 ♘c3 c6 8 ♗e3 ♗xe3 9 fxe3 ♘h6 10 ♖f1 ♕e7 11 ♕f3 d6 12 h3 ♗e6= Rambeau-Sallerin, Paris 1993;

b) 4 c3 ♘xf3+ 5 ♕xf3 ♘f6 6 d4 d6 7 ♗g5 ♗e7 8 h3 0-0 9 0-0+= Werner-Vuckovic, Lenk 1994;

c) 4 ♘xd4 exd4 5 d3 d6 6 c3 dxc3 7 ♘xc3 ♘f6 8 ♗g5 ♗e7 9 0-0 0-0 10 f4 c6 11 e5? ♘g4 12 ♗xe7 ♕xe7 13 ♕e2 dxe5 14 h3 ♕c5+ 15 ♔h1 ♘e3∓ Renaud-Toure, Elista 1998.

4 ... ♕g5 5 ♘xf7

If 5 ♘g4 White loses a piece to 5 ... d5! but 5 ♗xf7+ needs a considered response. 5 ... ♔d8! leaves White struggling. For instance: 6 0-0 ♕xe5 7 c3 ♘c6 8 d4 ♕f6 9 ♗xg8 ♖xg8 10 e5 ♕g6 (Tartakower) or 6 ♘g4 ♘h6! 7 c3 ♘c2+! 8 ♕xc2 ♕xg4 9 ♗c4 ♕xg2 10 ♖f1 ♘g4 intending ... ♘xh2 and 11 f3? is crunched by 11 ... ♘e3-+ (Bucker).

5 ... ♕xg2 6 ♘xh8

White has been well and truly tricked since the plausible-looking 6 ♖f1 allows 6 ... ♕xe4+ 7 ♗e2 ♘f3 mate.

6 ... ♕xh1+ 7 ♗f1 ♕xe4+ 8 ♗e2 d5 9 d3 ♘f3+ 10 ♔f1 ♗h3 mate

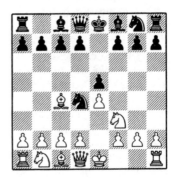

after 3 ... ♘d4

after 5 ♘xf7

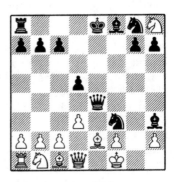

after 10 ... ♗h3 mate

Alekhine: 4 e6
Kobas-Shabalov
Philadelphia 1996

1 e4 ♘f6 2 ♘c3 d5 3 e5
3 d4 is a novel way of transposing
to the Blackmar-Diemer Gambit.
3 ... ♘fd7 4 e6?!
A speculative pawn sacrifice to
stifle Black's development.
4 ... fxe6 5 d4 c5
This is better than 5 ... g6 which
gives White a target. For instance: 6
h4 ♘f6 7 h5 ♘xh5 8 ♖xh5 gxh5 9
♕xh5+ ♔d7 10 ♘f3 ♕e8 (10 ...
♗g7 11 ♗h6 ♗f6 12 ♘xd5! exd5
13 ♕xd5+ ♔e8 14 ♕h5+ ♔d7 15
0-0-0 with a great attack) 11 ♕e5
♖g8 12 ♘xd5 ♕d8 13 ♘f4 ♗g7 14
♕xe6+ 1-0 Cheah-Dada, Manila
Olympiad 1992.
6 dxc5
a) 6 ♗d3 ♘f6 7 dxc5 ♘c6 8 ♗g5
g6 9 ♘h3 ♗g7 10 ♘f4 d4 11 ♘e4
e5 12 ♗xf6 exf6 13 ♘d6+ ♔f8 14
♘e2 ♕a5+ 15 ♕d2 ♕xc5-+ Jacobs-
Shabalov, Philadelphia 1997.
b) 6 ♘f3 ♘c6 7 ♗b5 e5?! (7 ...
g6!?) 8 dxe5 e6 9 ♘g5 ♘d4 10 ♕g4
♕e7 11 ♘xh7 ♘xc2+ 12 ♔d1
♘xa1 13 ♘xd5 exd5 14 ♗g5 ♕xe5
15 ♕h5+ 1-0 Hector-Konopka,
Bundesliga 1997.
6 ... ♘c6 7 ♘f3 a6
Because 7 ... ♘xc5 is met by 8
♗b5 with some play for the pawn.
**8 ♗e3 ♘f6 9 ♗d4 ♕c7 10 ♕d3
g6 11 0-0-0 ♗g7 12 h4? e5**
The threat is ... e5-e4.
13 ♘xe5 ♘xe5 14 ♕g3
If 14 ♕e2 White has not much for
the piece after 14 ... ♘f7 15 ♘xd5
♘xd5 16 ♗xg7 ♘f4 17 ♕e3 ♖g8.
**14 ... ♘e4 15 ♘xe4 dxe4 16 ♖e1
♘d3+ 0-1**

after 4 e6

after 7 ♘f3

after 12 ... e5

Elephant Gambit: 3 ♘xe5
Dodson-Rogers
Nottingham 1990

1 e4 e5 2 ♘f3 d5

Though played for years and years, the Elephant Gambit remains neglected in most opening books. However, Jonathan Rogers's discovery of many new ideas has recently led to a mini-revival.

3 ♘xe5

a) 3 c3 dxe4 4 ♕a4+ ♗d7 5 ♕xe4 ♘c6 6 ♘xe5? ♕e7 7 d4 f6-+ Choi-Shaughnessy, Elista 1998.

b) 3 exd5 ♗d6 (the older 3 ... e4 4 ♕e2 ♘f6 5 ♘c3 is good for White) 4 ♘c3 ♘f6 5 d3 h6 6 ♗e2 (6 g3!?) 6 ... 0-0 7 0-0 ♘bd7 8 d4 e4 9 N2 ♖e8 10 ♘c4 ♘b6 11 ♘xd6 ♕xd6 12 ♗e3 ♘bxd5 13 ♘xd5 ♘xd5 14 c4 ♘f4=+ Hyslop-Hebden, London Rapidplay 1995.

3 ... ♗d6

Cochrane-Staunton, London 1842 continued instead 3 ... ♕e7 4 d4 f6 5 ♘c3?! fxe5 6 ♘xd5 ♕f7 7 ♗c4 ♗e6 8 0-0 c6 9 f4 cxd5 10 fxe5 ♕d7? 11 exd5 ♗xd5 12 e6 ♕c6 13 ♕h5+ winning.

4 d4 dxe4 5 ♘c3 ♘f6 6 ♗g5 ♗f5 7 ♗c4 0-0 8 0-0 ♘bd7

Rogers is keen to exchange the central knight to increase the scope of his dark-squared bishop on the b8-h2 diagonal.

9 ♘xd7 ♕xd7 10 ♗xf6 gxf6 11 f3 ♖ae8 12 ♘xe4 ♗xe4 13 fxe4 ♖xe4 14 ♕h5 ♗xh2+!

It turns out that, despite the doubled f-pawns, the white king is more exposed than Black's.

15 ♔xh2 ♕xd4 16 g3 ♕xc4 17 ♖f2 ♖fe8 18 ♖af1 ♖e2 19 ♕f5 ♖8e6 20 ♔h3 ♖6e5 21 ♕xf6 ♖h5+ 22 ♔g2 ♕d5+ 23 ♕f3 ♖h2+ 0-1

after 2 ... d5

after 8 ... ♘bd7

after 23 ... ♖h2+

Conclusion

The impact of a new idea in the opening can be truly dramatic. There is no shortage of games where an unusual move backed up by a logical plan leads to an immediate collapse of the opponent's defence.

In Szenetra-Thiele White adopts a straightforward attacking plan and reaps the rewards—all because Black is unfamiliar with his opponent's formation and struggles in vain to find the right response.

But beware—there are exceptions too! In Kobas-Shabalov, White tries out a forgotten variation in an attempt to complicate matters, but his well-prepared opponent refutes the line and hangs on to the sacrificed pawn.

The Art of Attack

1 Choose an opening surprise that you think will be unsettling for a typical opponent.

2 Play the new idea at an early stage of the game so that your opponent will not have a chance to deviate from the prepared line.

3 Back up each idea with a plan and not just a one move trick.

The Art of Defence

1 Remain calm and don't panic—this is rule No.1! You need a little time to adjust to the change in circumstances.

2 Pounce upon and refute any dubious line.

3 Reject the offer to enter wild complications. Your opponent will probably be aware of the various tricks and traps—so side-step any preparation and find a solid reply.

9 Lack of Development

It makes sense to develop your pieces to their optimum squares so that they are handily placed for attack or defence. The centre pawns should be advanced to free the bishops and the queen; then, when the knights have been developed and the squares between the king and rook are vacant, you can contemplate castling and bringing the rooks into play. However, in practice, such a continuous development rarely occurs, since most opening variations tend to require the advance of several pawns, repeated moves with the same piece, or a need to deal with individual threats.

Dr Siegbert Tarrasch, a great chess player and teacher from the good old days, proclaimed that if one piece stands badly, all the pieces stand badly. These wise words are never truer than in the following games where the loser gets into difficulties because his pieces remain rooted to their original squares. An obvious example is Mah-Vukovic where Black comes under a direct attack straight out of the opening and is forced to resign before he has developed hardly any of his pieces. The game Taimanov-Polugaevsky shows how, even at top level, a tricky opening and some dazzling tactics can soon destroy a badly developed opponent.

If you think that no one falls for an opening trick once it has been published, then take a look at the number of people that have fallen victim to traps given here. This should convince you that it is possible to gain victory in the opening with relatively little knowledge.

Sacrificing at an early stage to take advantage of poor development is the theme of the game Ady-Waitzkin which underlines the difficulties of manoeuvring pieces when under attack—a defensive task which should never be underestimated. Pinter-Tkachiev shows a more subtle approach with Black gambiting a pawn simply for active play. In the end, White's inability to develop his kingside contributes greatly to his downfall.

'The threat is stronger than the execution' is a suitable slogan for the game Nunn-Kopec. Black feels so endangered by White's initiative that he lacks the confidence to castle. This upsets the coordination of his pieces to such an extent that he finds it impossible to defend himself along the open lines leading to his king. Meanwhile Miladinovic-Christenson shows how a slightly unusual opening can work wonders. Black falters at a critical early stage of the opening and falls for an unlikely mating attack.

Dutch: 3 d5
Miles-Vaisser
Elista Olympiad 1998

1 d4 e6 2 ♘f3 f5 3 d5

You will have a hard time finding analysis on this move in books on the Dutch Defence. Long considered a minor side-line, it has suddenly become popular. The main idea is to stop Black adopting his favourite Stonewall pawn formation with ... d5.

3 ... exd5

Others:

a) 3 ... ♗d6 4 dxe6 dxe6 5 e4 fxe4 6 ♘g5 ♗b4+ 7 c3 ♕xd1+ 8 ♔xd1 ♗e7 9 ♘xe4 ♘f6 10 ♗d3 ♘c6 11 ♘bd2 ♗d7 12 ♖e1 ♘e5 13 ♗f1 ♘f7 14 ♔c2 gave White the slightly better chances thanks to Black's weak e6 pawn in Hauchard-Roos, French Championship 1994.

b) 3 ... ♗b4+ 4 c3 (4 ♗d2 ♕e7 5 c4 ♘f6 6 ♘c3 is an interesting alternative for White) 4 ... ♗d6 5 g3 ♘f6 6 dxe6 dxe6 7 ♘bd2 0-0 8 ♘c4 ♕e7 9 ♗f4 ♗xf4 10 gxf4 b6 11 ♗g2 ♗b7 12 0-0 ♘bd7 13 ♘fe5= Ward-Holst, Copenhagen 1998.

4 ♕xd5 d6 5 ♘g5 ♕e7 6 ♘xh7!

The point of the preceding moves is revealed. White wins a pawn but must now allow his queen to be chased around the board if he wants to hang on to the extra material.

6 ... c6 7 ♕b3 ♖xh7

If 7 ... ♗e6 then 8 ♕g3, threatening 9 ♕g6+, is good for White.

8 ♕xg8 ♖h4

Now the threat is ... ♗e6 to trap the queen.

9 ♕b3 ♘a6

In the game Agrest-Karlsson, Stockholm 1997, Black tried a direct attack on the white queen with

after 3 d5

after 5 ♘g5

after 9 ... ♘a6

9 ... ♗e6. The continuation was 10 ♕c3 g5 11 g3 ♗g7 12 ♕d2 ♖h5 13 ♘c3 ♘d7 14 ♗g2 d5 with attacking chances for Black. However, I believe there is a big improvement for White by playing 10 ♗g5! which neutralises Black's initiative. For example: 10 ... ♗xb3 11 ♗xe7 ♗xe7 12 axb3 leaves White a pawn up in the ending or 10 ... ♕f7 11 ♕d3/11 ♕a3 and White has the better chances.

10 ♕e3 ♖e4!?

It might be better to adopt a more restrained policy by playing 10 ... ♗e6 to avoid the exchange of queens.

11 ♕d2 ♘b4 12 ♕d1

An incredible position which seems to defy most of the positional rules of chess. Miles has grabbed a pawn and is now hoping to rebuff Black's attack by means of c3 followed by ♘d2-f3. Vaisser's biggest problem is to stop smiling!

12 ... ♖d4 13 ♘d2 f4 14 a3

14 c3 forks two pieces and also allows 14 ... ♘d3 mate!

14 ... ♘d5 15 c3 ♘e3!

The only way to save the rook as 15 ... ♖d3 loses after 16 ♕c2 ♗f5 17 ♔d1.

16 fxe3 ♕h4+ 17 g3 fxg3 18 ♗g2 gxh2+!

The imaginative 18 ... ♗h3 fails to impress after 19 exd4 ♗xg2 20 ♘f3! ♗xf3 21 exf3 g2+ 22 ♔e2 gxh1=♕ 23 ♕xh1 when White remains a pawn up without having to fear a vicious attack.

19 ♔f1 ♕f6+ 20 ♔e1

Not 20 ♗f3?? ♗h3+ 21 ♔f2 ♕h4 mate.

20 ... ♕h4+ 21 ♔f1 ½-½

after 12 ♕d1

after 15 ... ♘e3

after 19 ... ♕f6+

QGD Tarrasch: 5 e4
Mah-Vuckovic
European U-16s, Zagan 1995

1 d4 d5 2 c4 e6 3 ♘c3 c5 4 cxd5 exd5 5 e4

An ambitious line which seeks to put Black under pressure by bombarding him with tactics.

5 ... dxe4

The choice in the stem game of this variation was 5 ... ♘c6 which continued 6 exd5 ♘xd4 7 ♘f3 (7 ♘ge2!?) 7 ... ♘xf3+ 8 ♕xf3 ♗d6 9 ♗b5+ ♗d7 10 0-0 ♘e7 11 ♗g5 0-0= Marshall-Schlechter, Monte Carlo 1904.

6 ♗c4

After 6 d5 Black survives after 6 ... f5 7 ♗f4 ♗d6 8 ♗b5+ ♔f7 9 ♘h3 ♘f6 10 ♗c4 a6 11 a4 h6=+.

6 ... cxd4?

He should pay more attention to his development and try 6 ... ♘c6, e.g. 7 d5 ♘e5 8 ♘xe4 ♘xc4 9 ♕a4+ ♗d7 10 ♕xc4 ♕e7 11 ♗g5 f6 12 ♗e3 b5 13 ♕d3 c4 14 ♕d4 ♕e5 with equal chances as in Summerscale-Gershon, Tel Aviv 1997.

7 ♕b3! ♕e7?

a) 7 ... dxc3? 8 ♗xf7+ ♔d7 9 ♗f4 ♕b6 10 ♖d1+ ♔e7 11 ♗d6+ ♔f6 12 ♗e5+! ♔e7 13 ♗xg8 ♕xb3 14 ♗xb3 cxb2 15 ♗xb2 gives White compensation for the pawn.

b) 7 ... ♕d7 is still in White's favour after 8 ♘xe4 ♕e7 9 ♔f1.

8 ♘d5 ♕d7 9 ♗f4 ♗d6 10 ♕g3 ♗xf4 11 ♕xf4 ♔d8 12 ♕e5 ♘c6

12 ... f5 is necessary to defend g7 when 13 ♕xd4 ♘f6 14 0-0-0 gives White the better game.

13 ♕xg7 ♕g4 14 ♕f8+ ♔d7 15 ♕xf7+ ♔d8 16 ♕c7+ ♔e8 17 ♕d6 1-0

after 5 e4

after 9 ♗f4

after 12 ♕e5

QGD: 4 ♕a4+
Taimanov-Polugaevsky
USSR Championship 1960

1 d4 d5 2 c4 dxc4 3 ♘f3 ♘f6 4 ♕a4+ ♘bd7

It is possible to transpose to main lines after 4 ... ♘c6 or 4 ... c6 by playing 5 ♕xc4. Also possible:

a) 4 ... ♕d7 5 ♕xc4 ♕c6 6 ♘bd2 ♗e6 7 ♕xc6+ ♘xc6 8 a3 (8 ♗b5) 8 ... 0-0-0 9 e3 ♗d5 10 b4 ♘e4 11 ♘xe4 ♗xe4 12 ♗b2 a6 13 ♗e2= Fedorowicz-Shirazi, USA Ch 1984.

b) 4 ... ♗d7 5 ♕xc4 e6 6 ♗g5 ♗c6 7 ♘c3 ♗xf3 8 gxf3 c6 9 e3 ♘bd7 10 ♗e2 ♗e7 11 ♗h4 0-0 12 ♗g3 a6 13 0-0 ♖c8 14 ♖fd1 c5 15 dxc5 b5 16 ♕d3 ♘xc5 17 ♕xd8 ♖fxd8 18 ♖ac1= Piket-Nikolic, Linares 1997.

5 ♘c3 e6 6 e4 c5 7 d5

It should be noted that this position can arise from a variety of move-orders such as 1 d4 ♘f6 2 c4 e6 3 ♘f3 d5 4 ♘c3 dxc4 5 ♕a4+ ♘bd7 6 e4 c5 7 d5 or 1 d4 d5 2 ♘f3 ♘f6 3 c4 dxc4 4 ♘c3 e6 5 ♕a4+ ♘bd7 6 e4 c5 7 d5.

7 ... exd5 8 e5 d4

Keres suggested 8 ... b5 which is probably the only way for Black to avoid disaster. One way to continue is with 9 ♕xb5 ♖b8 10 ♕a4 d4 11 exf6 dxc3 12 ♗xc4 ♖b4! (12 ... cxb2? allows a brilliant finish after 13 ♗xf7+! ♔xf7 14 ♘g5+ ♔xf6 15 ♕c6+ ♔f5 16 ♕e6 mate) 13 ♕d1 ♘xf6 14 ♗xf7+ ♔e7 15 ♕xd8+ ♔xd8 16 bxc3 ♖e4+ 17 ♗e3 ♔e7 18 ♗b3 ♘g4 when White is slightly better according to an analysis by Ftacnik.

9 ♗xc4 dxc3 10 exf6 ♕xf6

It a hopeless case for Black to try and wriggle out of the dire situation

after 4 ♕a4+

after 8 e5

after 11 ... ♕c6

with 10 ... gxf6. I was lured into this dreadful position against Kinsman at Wrexham 1997 and soon succumbed upon 11 0-0 ♗g7 12 ♖e1+ ♔f8 13 ♗f4 ♘e5 14 ♖ad1 ♕e7 15 bxc3 ♗g4 16 ♗d5 ♗d7 17 ♕e4 ♖e8 18 ♘h4+-. I quickly found out from my opponent why the game was watched with particular interest by Taimanov!

11 ♗g5 ♕c6 12 0-0-0!

A fantastic decision—abandoning the queen to allow the rooks to enter the attack. A clear case of the perils of poor development.

12 ... cxb2+

The queen is taboo as 12 ... ♕xa4 loses after 13 ♖he1+ ♗e7 14 ♖xe7+ ♔f8 15 ♖xf7+ ♔g8 16 ♖fxd7+ ♕xc4 17 ♖d8+ ♔f7 18 ♘e4+ ♔xe6 19 ♘xc4+-. The only other move that represents a chance for Black is 12 ... ♗e7. However, the game Garcia Palermo-Gelfand, Oakham 1988, will hardly inspire confidence. The game continued: 13 ♕xc6 bxc6 14 ♗xe7 cxb2+ 15 ♔xb2 ♔xe7 16 ♖he1+ ♔d8 17 ♘e5 ♔c7 18 ♘xd7 ♗xd7 19 ♖e7 ♖ad8 20 ♗xf7 ♖hf8 21 f3 1-0.

13 ♔xb2 ♗e7 14 ♖he1 f6 15 ♗b5

All of White's pieces are poised for the onslaught.

15 ... ♕b6 16 ♔c1 fxg5 17 ♗xd7+ ♔f8 18 ♖xe7!

The most efficient way to end the game.

18 ... ♔xe7 19 ♕e4+ ♔d8 20 ♗f5+ ♔c7 21 ♕e5+ ♔c6 22 ♖d6+ ♔b5 23 ♕b2+ 1-0

after 15 ♗b5

after 18 ... ♔e7

after 23 ♕b2+

Sicilian: Kalashnikov
Ady-Waitzkin
New York 1998

1 e4 c5 2 ♘f3 ♘c6 3 d4 cxd4 4 ♘xd4 e5 5 ♘b5 d6

An enterprising variation which differs from the more familiar Sveshnikov in that the king's knight can be moved to e7 rather f6. This move-order makes it awkward for White to judge the correct plan.

6 ♘1c3

This tactical approach is typical of Ady's aggressive style. 6 c4 is the positional move, in order to gain space on the queenside and secure the d5 square.

6 ... a6 7 ♘a3 b5 8 ♘d5 ♘ce7

A speciality of Waitzkin.

9 ♗g5 h6 10 ♗xb5+!?

A calculated gamble to try and take advantage of Black's dormant pieces.

10 ... axb5 11 ♘xb5 ♖a6 12 ♘dc7+ ♔d7 13 ♗d2

White wants to take the rook on a6 without allowing 13 ... ♕a5+.

13 ♕d2 is also playable. Edelman-Khan, Philadelphia 1998, ended in a brilliant victory after 13 ♕d2 hxg5 14 ♘xa6 ♕b6 15 ♘ac7 ♘f6 16 0-0-0 ♘c6 17 ♕xg5 ♘d4 18 a4 ♘xe4 19 ♕g4+ f5 20 ♕g6 ♘f6 21 ♕f7+ ♗e7 22 ♖xd4 ♖f8 23 ♕e6+ ♔d8 24 ♕xe5 1-0.

13 ... ♖b6

It might be better to consider 13 ... ♖c6 but White still has a strong initiative.

14 c4 ♗a6?

Black cracks under the pressure. The threat of c4-c5 suggests 14 ... ♖c6.

15 ♗a5 ♗xb5 16 ♗xb6 ♗c6 17 c5 ♘f6 18 ♘a6 1-0

after 5 ... d6

after 9 ... h6

after 14 c4

Sicilian: Richter-Rauzer
Nunn-Kopec
British National League 1998

1 e4 c5 2 ♘f3 d6 3 d4 cxd4 4 ♘xd4 ♘f6 5 ♘c3 ♘c6 6 ♗g5 e6 7 ♕d2 a6 8 0-0-0 ♗d7 9 f3
By adopting this rarely seen line Nunn avoids the mass of theory associated with 9 f4. White's basic idea is to keep his options open and contemplate a kingside pawn storm with h4 and g4.

9 ... ♘xd4
The game Nunn-Ydeslaver, Leeuwarden 1995, saw 9 ... ♗e7 which is a popular reply: 10 h4 ♖c8 11 ♔b1 h6 12 ♘xc6 ♗xc6 13 ♗e3 d5 14 e5 ♘d7 15 f4 ♗xh4 16 ♗d4 ♗e7 17 ♕f2 b5 18 f5 with a terrific attack.

10 ♕xd4 b5 11 f4
Black has developed his queenside swiftly but at the cost of leaving his king in the middle of the board. This inspires Nunn to open up the centre.

11 ... ♗e7 12 e5 dxe5 13 fxe5 ♘d5 14 ♗xe7 ♘xe7 15 ♗d3 ♕c7
It is already difficult for Kopec to harmonise his pieces because 15 ... 0-0 is well met by 16 ♗xh7+! ♔xh7 17 ♕xd7.

16 ♘e4 ♘f5 17 ♕f2 ♕xe5?!
In a difficult position the lure of a free pawn proves too much. The alternative 17 ... 0-0 18 g4 ♘e7 19 ♘d6 ♗c6 20 ♖hf1 is better for White.

18 g4 ♘h6 19 ♖he1 ♗c6 20 ♗xb5! ♕c7
If 20 ... axb5 then 21 ♘d6+ wins the queen.

21 ♘d6+ 1-0
Black resigned in view of 21 ... ♔f8 22 ♕c5! axb5 23 ♘f5+ ♔g8 24 ♘e7+ ♔f8 25 ♘d5+ wins.

after 9 f3

after 15 ♗d3

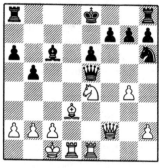

after 19 ... ♗c6

Pirc: 150 Attack
Lane-Bernard
Huy 1992

1 e4 d6 2 d4 ♘f6 3 ♘c3 g6 4 ♗e3 ♗g7 5 ♕d2

The slight difference between this and other ♗e3 lines is that here White retains the option of f3, rather than ♘f3, to accelerate the attack. This line is very popular with English amateurs who chose the name '150' because, according to the old fashioned English grading system, this is the strength of a decent club player. A translation to Elo would be the less colourful '1800 Attack'.

5 ... c6

Black wants to distract White from launching an imminent kingside attack by instigating queenside play. In the game Lane-Miles, Le Touquet 1990, I met 5 ... ♘c6 with 6 f3 to help a kingside pawn storm and soon had a powerful attack: 6 ... 0-0 7 0-0-0 e5 8 ♘ge2 ♗d7 9 ♔b1 ♕b8? 10 g4 b5 11 ♗h6 ♗xh6 12 ♕xh6 ♘xd4 13 g5! ♘e8 14 ♘xd4 exd4 15 ♘d5 f5 16 ♘e7+ ♔f7 17 ♕xh7+ ♘g7 18 exf5+-.

6 ♗h6 ♗xh6 7 ♕xh6 ♕a5 8 ♗d3 ♘bd7 9 ♘f3 ♕h5

Black would be happy to swap queens to avoid the attack.

10 ♕d2 ♕a5 11 ♕h6 ♕h5 12 ♕f4 ♘b6 13 a4 ♕g4 14 ♕e3 ♕xg2

A hot pawn but otherwise the queen will be chased around the board anyway. Black's main problem is that his development is poor and White is threatening to open up the centre.

15 ♖g1 ♕h3 16 a5 ♘bd7 17 ♖g3 ♕h5 18 ♖g5 ♕h6 19 e5 ♘d5 20 ♘xd5 cxd5 21 exd6 e6 22 0-0-0 0-0 23 ♖xg6+! 1-0

after 5 ♕d2

after 9 ... ♕h5

after 21 ... 0-0

King's Indian: 5 h3
Pinter-Tkachiev
Porec 1998

**1 d4 ♘f6 2 c4 g6 3 ♘c3 ♗g7 4
e4 d6 5 h3 0-0 6 ♗g5**

It is always good to know when an opening line has been busted! Anyone who has memorised the second edition of *ECO E* will be in for a shock if they follow the recommendation there, 6 ♘f3 ♘bd7 7 e5 ♘e8 8 ♗f4 c6 9 ♕d2 dxe5 10 dxe5 ♘c7 11 ♖d1 ♘e6 12 ♗h6 ♕a5 13 ♗xg7 ♔xg7 14 ♕e3+=, since Nunn has pointed out the improvement of 12 ... ♘xe5! when 13 ♘xe5 ♕xd2+ or 13 ♕xd8 ♘xf3+ leaves Black is a pawn up.

**6 ... ♘bd7 7 ♗d3 c5 8 d5 ♘e5 9
♗e2**

In such a blocked position the value of the light-squared bishop is diminished so White should prefer 9 ♘f3 instead.

9 ... b5!

At the first sign of indecision Tkachiev grabs the chance to steal the initiative.

**10 cxb5 a6 11 bxa6 ♕a5 12 ♗d2
♗xa6 13 ♕c2 ♖fb8 14 ♖b1 ♘fd7**

At the cost of a pawn, Black has active piece play whereas Pinter's kingside development is woeful.

**15 f4 ♘c4 16 ♗xc4 ♗xc4 17 b3
♗xc3!**

Black spots a clever combination to break through on the queenside.

**18 ♗xc3 ♕xa2 19 ♖b2 ♕a1+ 20
♔f2 ♕f1+ 21 ♔e3 ♖a3!**

The exposed white king enables Tkachiev to carry out a triumphant finale.

22 bxc4 ♖xb2 23 ♕xb2 ♘b6 0-1

after 5 ... 0-0

after 9 ... b5

after 21 ♔e3

Pseudo-Trompowsky: 2 ... h6
Miladinovic-Christenson
Korinthos 1998

1 d4 d5 2 ♗g5

This move was routinely played by Hodgson at a time when most people considered it a joke. His success was quickly copied by Adams and it is now regarded as a fearsome weapon.

2 ... h6

A sly move-order. Black nudges the bishop out of the way so that after ... ♕b6 is played the bishop is unable to fend off checks on the e1-a5 diagonal or even retreat to c1.

3 ♗h4 c6 4 e3

I prefer this practical approach to 4 ♘f3 after which can follow 4 ... ♕b6 5 b3 ♗f5 6 e3 ♘d7 7 ♗d3 ♗xd3 8 ♕xd3 e6= as in Anand-Karpov, FIDE World Championship, Lausanne 1998. The difference is that 5 ♕c1 is no longer possible because then 5 ... g5 6 ♗g3 g4 would simply win the d-pawn.

4 ... ♕b6 5 ♕c1 e5

An energetic way to fight for a space advantage.

6 ♘f3

If 6 dxe5?? then 6 ... ♕b4+ winning the bishop on h4. The game Siegel-Nor, Budapest 1997, saw 5 ... ♗f5 which allowed White to expand on the queenside with a standard plan: 6 ♘f3 ♘d7 7 c4 ♗xb1 8 ♖xb1 e6 9 c5 ♕c7 10 ♗g3 ♕c8 11 b4+=.

6 ... e4 7 ♘fd2 ♗e6 8 c4 ♘d7 9 ♘c3 ♖c8? 10 cxd5 cxd5 11 ♘xd5!

White abandons his queen in search of mate.

11 ... ♕c6

11 ... ♖xc1+ 12 ♖xc1 ♗xd5 13 ♖c8+ mates.

12 ♕xc6 bxc6 13 ♗a6 1-0

after 2 ♗g5

after 5 ♕c1

after 11 ♘xd5

Conclusion

Though failing to develop one's pieces is responsible for many a defeat, there are exceptions. In Miles-Vaisser, White wins a pawn and then finds his queen pushed around the board until it has to return to its original square. A comical position arises in which it looks like Miles has already started setting up the pieces for the next game! However Black cannot quite force a win and settles for a draw by perpetual check.

Nevertheless there is no doubt that having more pieces in play does enable a player to take the initiative and launch an early attack. This is especially true in a sharp opening variation such as that seen in Lane-Bernard, where I not only gained a space advantage, which is usual against the Pirc, but also an advantage in development by continually attacking a wandering black queen with gain of time.

The Art of Attack

1 Look for ways to attack if your opponent's position shows signs of poor development.

2 Before deciding on a sacrificial breakthrough, assess the opponent's ability to defend. If his forces are still on their original squares then the odds should be in your favour.

3 Lack of development may be a sign that your opponent is foundering in an unfamiliar or very tactical opening variation. The solution? Attack!

The Art of Defence

1 Be wary of accepting material if it means you lose several tempi. Backward development is often the key element in the success of an enemy attack.

2 Avoid moving the same piece twice in the opening if this results in slower development.

3 Choose an opening to suit your style. Some variations disregard continuous development in search of quick counterplay or gain in material. These risky lines may well be safely adopted by top-class grandmasters but most of us mere mortals have to be a little more careful!

Index of games